CW01501585

Mansur Hallaj

Selected Poems

A Selection by the same Author

[See back pages of this book for descriptions of some]

TRANSLATIONS: Divan of Hafiz, Hafiz: The Oracle, Ruba'iyat of Hafiz, Hafiz: Tongue of the Hidden, Hafiz: Book of the Winebringer, Hafiz: Love's Perfect Gift, Hafiz: Selected Poems, Seven Hundred Sayings of Kabir, Ruba'iyat of Rumi, Ruba'iyat of Sadi, Rumi: Selected Poems, Divan of Sadi, Nizami: Layla and Majnun, Nizami: Treasury of the Mysteries, Nizami: Selected Poems, Obeyd Zakani: The Dervish Joker, Obeyd Zakani's Mouse & Cat, Hafiz's Friend: Jahan Khatun, Piercing Pearls: The Complete Anthology of Persian Poetry (2 vols.); Princesses, Sufis, Dervishes, Martyrs and Feminists: Eight Women Poets of the East, Makhfi: The Princess Sufi Poet Zeb-un-Nissa, The Sufi Ruba'iyat: An Anthology, The Sufi & Dervish Ghazal: An Anthology, The Ruba'iyat: A World Anthology, The Ghazal: A World Anthology, The Divine Wine: A Treasury of Sufi & Dervish Poetry (2 vols.), The Masnavi: A World Anthology, The Qasida: A World Anthology, Ibn al-Farid: Wine & The Mystic's Progress, Unity in Diversity: Anthology of Sufi Poets of Indian Sub-Continent; Tongues on Fire: Anthology of the Poets of Afghanistan; Wine, Blood & Roses: Anthology of Turkish Poets, Love's Agony & Bliss: Anthology of Urdu Poetry; Hearts With Wings: Anthology of Persian Sufi & Dervish Poetry, Breezes of Truth: Selected Arabic Sufi Poetry, Yunus Emre, Turkish Dervish: Selected Poems, Anthology of Classical Arabic Poetry, The Qit'a: Anthology of the 'Fragment' in Arabic, Persian & Eastern Poetry, Ruba'iyat of al-Ma'arri, Ruba'iyat of Sarmad, Ruba'iyat of 'Attar, Ruba'iyat of Abu Said, Ruba'iyat of Mahsati, Ruba'iyat of Baba Tahir, Ruba'iyat of Jahan Khatun, Ruba'iyat of Sana'i, Sana'i: Selected Poems, The Poets of Shiraz, Ruba'iyat of Jami, Jami: Selected Poems, Ruba'iyat of Khayyam, Ruba'iyat of Auhad ud-din, Huma: Selected Poems of Meher Baba, Rudaki: Selected Poems, The Seven Golden Odes (Qasidas) of Arabia, The Qita: Anthology of 'Fragment' in Arabic, Persian and Eastern Poetry, Ruba'iyat of Nesimi, Nesimi: Selected Poems, Ruba'iyat of Bedil, Bedil: Selected Poems, Anvari: Selected Poems, Ruba'iyat of 'Iraqi, The Wisdom of Ibn Yamin, Shabistari: The Rose Garden of Mystery, Shimmering Jewels: Anthology of Poetry under the Mughal Emperors of India (1526-1857), Amir Khusrau: Selected Poems, Rahman Baba: Selected Poems, Ruba'iyat of Dara Shikoh, Ruba'iyat of Ansari, Poems of Majnun (Qays), Mu'in ud-din Chishti: Selected Poems, Anthology of Poets of the Chishti Sufi Order, A Wealth of Poets: Persian Poetry at the Courts of Sultan Mahmud in Ghazneh & Sultan Sanjar in Ghanjeh (998-1158), Shah Ni'matullah Vali: Selected Poems, Ruba'iyat of Ni'matullah, Poets of the Ni'matullah Sufi Order, Ansari: Selected Poems, Baba Farid: Selected Poems., Qasidah Burdah: The Three Poems of the Prophet's Mantle, 'Iraqi: Selected Poems, 'Attar: Selected Poems, Ruba'iyat of Anvari, Zarathushtra: Selected Poems, Khushal Khan Khattak: The Great Warrior & poet of Afghanistan, Selected Poems.

FICTION: Hafiz of Shiraz: A Novel-Biography (3 vols), The First Mystery, The Second Mystery, Hafiz: The Ugly Little Boy Who Became a Great Poet, Pan of the Never-Never, The Greatest Game, The Healer and the Emperor, Golf is Murder, The Zen Golf Murder, Riana, The Greatest Game, Going Back.

POETRY: Pune: The City of God, Cradle Mountain, Pie Anthology (Editor); The Master, The Muse & The Poet: An Autobiography in Poetry; A Bird in His Hand, Compassionate Rose, The Cross of God. SCREENPLAYS: Hafiz of Shiraz, Layla & Majnun, Riana, The Castlemaine Kiss, The Greatest Game, The Healer & The Emperor, Golf is Murder, The Zen-Golf Murder, Pan of The Never-Never, Going Back. STAGE: Hafiz of Shiraz, Hafiz: The Musical. RADIO: The Sun of Shiraz. DANCE: The Eternal Triangle (with Meher Baba). TELEVISION: The Mark, The First Mystery, Pan of The Never-Never, Hafiz: The Series.

2

Mansur Hallaj

Selected Poems

Translations and Introduction

Paul Smith

NEW HUMANITY BOOKS
Book Heaven
Booksellers & Publishers

Copyright © Paul Smith 2012.

NEW HUMANITY BOOKS
BOOK HEAVEN
(Booksellers & Publishers for over 40 years)
47 Main Road Campbells Creek
Victoria, 3450 Australia

www.newhumanitybookbookheaven.com

ISBN: 978-1479346554

The Torture of Hallaj 'to relieve him of his demons'.

>CONTENTS<

The Life, Times and Works of Mansur Hallaj.

Husayn Mansur al-Hallaj (859-922) was a Perfect Master *(Qutub)* and a poet who was born near Shiraz (Bayda), Persia… a writer and teacher of Sufism most famous for his self-proclaimed divinity in his poetry and for his execution for heresy at the hands of the Abbasid rulers. Although Hallaj was born in Persia and was of Persian descent, he wrote most of his works in Arabic.

He married and had three children and made a pilgrimage to Mecca, stayed for one year, facing the mosque, in fasting and total silence. After his stay at the city, he traveled extensively and wrote and taught along the way. He traveled as far as India and Central Asia gaining many followers, many of whom accompanied him on his second and third trips to Mecca. After this period of travel, he settled in the capital of Baghdad.

During his early lifetime he was a disciple of Junaid and Amr al-Makki, but was later rejected by them both. Among other Sufis, Hallaj was an anomaly. Many Sufi masters felt that it was inappropriate to share his inner experiences with the masses, yet Mansur Hallaj openly did so in his writings and through his teachings. He began to make enemies, and the rulers saw him as a threat. This was exacerbated by times when he would fall into trances that he attributed to being in the presence of God. During one of these trances, he would utter *Anal-Haqq* literally meaning, "I am the Absolute Truth", which was taken to mean that he was claiming to be God. In another controversial statement, Hallaj claimed: "There is nothing wrapped in my turban but God," and, again, similarly, he would point to his cloak and say, "There is nothing inside my cloak except God."

These utterances led him to a long trial, and subsequent imprisonment for eleven years in a Baghdad prison. In the end, he was tortured and publicly crucified (in some accounts he was beheaded and his hands and feet were cut off) by the Abbasid rulers for what they deemed 'theological error threatening the security of the state.' Many accounts tell of Hallaj's calm demeanour even while he was being tortured, and indicate that he forgave those who had executed him. He was executed on March 26, 922. It is said that while he was savagely tortured before he was killed he kept calling out: *"Anal Haqq!"*

It is also reported that after his body was burnt and the ashes thrown into the Tigris River they spelt out the words *"Anal Haqq!"* His influence on all Sufis, be they poets or not, who have come after him, cannot be overestimated. (See Appendix).

Apart from the many books and poems that have been written and inspired by Sufism's greatest martyr in the past hundred years there have also been a number of plays and films and even puppet shows about his life and in particular his terrible death.

A Recent Play   An Iranian Puppet Play

Farid-ud-din 'Attar in his *Tazkirat-ul-Aulia* (*Muslim, Saints and Mystics*) says of him as follows:

"This is he who was a martyr in the way of truth, whose rank has become exalted, whose outer and inner man were pure, who has been a pattern of loyalty in love, whom an irresistible longing drew towards the contemplation of the face of God; this is the enthusiast Mansur Hallaj, may the mercy of God be upon him! He was intoxicated with a love whose flames consumed him. The miracles he worked were such that the learned were thunderstruck at them. He was a man whose range of vision was immense, whose words were riddles, and profoundly versed in the knowledge of mysteries. Born in the canton of Bayda in the province of Shiraz, he grew up at Wasit.

Abd Allah Khafif used to say, 'Mansur really possessed the knowledge of the truth.' 'I and Mansur,' declared Shibli, 'followed the same path; they regarded me as mad and my life was saved thereby, while Mansur perished because he was sane.' If Mansur had been really astray in error, the two learned men we have just quoted would not have spoken of him in such terms. Many wise men, however, have reproached him for revealing the mysteries of truth to the vulgar herd.

When he had grown up, he was two years in the service of Abd Allah Teshtari. He made the pilgrimage to Mecca, and on his return became a disciple of the Sufi Junaid. One day, when Mansur was plying him with questions on certain obscure and difficult points, Junaid said, 'O Mansur, before very long you will redden the head of the stake.'

'The day when I redden the head of the stake,' rejoined Mansur, 'you will cast away the garment of the dervish and assume that of ordinary men.' It is related that on the day when Mansur was taken to execution all the Ulama (head priests) signed the sentence of death. 'Junaid also must sign,' said the Caliph. Junaid accordingly repaired to the college of the Ulama, where, after putting on a mullah's robe and turban, he recorded in writing his opinion that 'though apparently Mansur deserved death, inwardly he possessed the knowledge of the Most High.'

Having left Bagdad, Mansur spent a year at Tashter, then he spent five years in travelling through Khorassan, Seistan and Turkestan. On his return to Bagdad, the number of his followers largely increased, and he gave utterance to many strange sayings which excited the suspicions of the orthodox. At last he began to say, 'I am the Truth.' These words were repeated to the Caliph and many persons renounced Mansur as a religious leader and appeared as witnesses against him. Among these was Junaid, to whom the Caliph said, 'O Junaid, what is the meaning of this saying of Mansur?' 'O Caliph,' answered Junaid, 'this man should be put to death, for such a saying cannot be reasonably explained.' The Caliph then ordered him to be cast into prison. There for a whole year he continued to hold discussions with the learned. At the end of that time the Caliph forbade that anyone should have access to him; in consequence, no one went to see him for five months except Abd Allah Khafif. Another time Ibn Ata sent someone to say to him, 'O Sheikh, withdraw what you said, so that you may escape death.' 'No, rather he who sent you to me should ask forgiveness,' replied Mansur. Ibn Ata, hearing this, shed tears and said, 'Alas, he is irreparably lost!'

In order to force him to retract, he was first of all given three hundred blows with a rod, but in vain. He was then led to execution. A crowd of about a hundred thousand men followed him and as he looked around on them, he cried, 'True! True! True! I am the Truth!'

It is said that among them was a dervish who asked him, 'What is love?'

'You will see,' Mansur replied, 'to-day and to-morrow and the day after.' And as it happened, that day he was put to death, the next day his body was burnt and on the third his ashes were scattered to the winds. He meant that such would be the results of his love to God. On his son asking of him a last piece of advice he said, 'While the people of the world spend their energies on earthly objects, you apply yourself to a study, the least portion of which is worth all that men and *jinn* can produce... the study of truth.'

As he walked along lightly and alertly, though loaded with many chains, they asked him the reason of his confident bearing. 'It is,' he said, 'because I am going to the presence of the King.' Then he added, 'My Host, in whom there is no injustice, has presented me with the drink which is usually given to a guest; but when the cups have began to circulate he has sent for the executioner with his sword and leathern carpet. Thus fares it with him who drinks with the Dragon in July.'

When he reached the scaffold, he turned his face towards the western gate of Bagdad and set his foot on the first rung of the ladder, 'the first step heavenward,' as he said. Then he girded himself with a girdle, and, lifting up his hands towards heaven, turned towards Mecca, and said exultantly, 'Let it be as He has willed.' When he reached the platform of the scaffold, a group of his disciples called out to him, 'What do you say regarding us, your disciples, and regarding those who deny your claims and are about to stone you?' 'They will have a two-fold reward, and you only a single one,' he answered, 'for you limit 'yourselves to having a good opinion of me, while they are carried on by their zeal for the unity of God and for the written law. Now in the law the doctrine of God's unity is fundamental, while a good opinion is merely accessory.'

Shibli the Sufi stood in front of him and cried, 'Did we not tell you not to gather men together?' Then he added, 'O Hallaj, what is Sufism?' 'Thou see,' replied Hallaj, 'the least part of it.' 'What is then the highest?' asked Shibli. 'You cannot attain to it,' he answered.

Then they all began to stone him. Shibli making common cause with the others threw mud at him. Hallaj uttered a cry. 'What,' said one, 'you have not flinched under this hail of stones and now you cry out because of a little mud! Why is that?' 'Ah!' he replied, 'they do not know what they are doing, and are excusable; but he grieves me because he knows I ought not to be stoned at all.'

When they cut off his hands he laughed and said, 'To cut off the hands of a fettered man is easy, but to sever the links which bind me to the Divinity would be a task indeed.' Then they cut off his two feet. He said smiling, 'With these I used to accomplish my earthly journeys, but I have another pair of feet with which I can traverse both worlds. Cut these off if you can!' Then, with his bleeding stumps, he rubbed his cheeks and arms. 'Why do you do that?' he was asked. 'I have lost much blood,' he answered, 'and lest you should think the pallor of my countenance shows fear, I have reddened my cheeks.' 'But why your arms?' 'The ablutions of love must be made in blood,' he replied.

Then his eyes were torn out. At this a tumult arose in the crowd. Some burst into tears, others cast stones at him. When they were about to cut out his tongue, he exclaimed, 'Wait a little; I have something to say.'

Then, lifting his face towards heaven, he said, 'My God, for the sake of these sufferings, which they inflict on me because of You, do not inflict loss upon them nor deprive them of their share of felicity. Behold, upon the scaffold of my torture I enjoy the contemplation of Your glory.' His last words were, 'Help me, O You only One, to whom there is no second!' and he recited the following verse of the *Koran*, 'Those who do not believe say, "Why does not the day of judgment hasten? Those who believe tremble at the mention of it, for they know that it is near."' Then they cut out his tongue, and he smiled. Finally, at the time of evening prayer, his head was cut off. His body was burnt, and the ashes thrown into the Tigris."

Translated by Claud Field in his *Mystics & Saints of Islam*, Francis Griffiths, London, 1910.

Abu 'l-Hasan al-Hujwiri (d. 1072) one of the most respected early authors on Sufism states in his *Kashf al-Mahjub* as translated by R.A. Nicholson… "He was an enamoured and intoxicated votary of Sufism. He had a strong ecstasy and a lofty spirit. The Sufi Shaykhs are at variance concerning him. Some reject him, while others accept him. Among the latter class are He was an enamoured and intoxicated votary of

Sufism. Among the latter class are Amr b. Uthman al- Makki, Abu Ya'qub Nahrajuri, Abu Ya'qub Aqta', Ali b. Sahl Isfahani, and others. He is accepted, moreover, by Ibn 'Ata, Muhammad b. Khafif, Abu 'l-Qasim Nasrabadi, and all the moderns. Others, again, suspend their judgment about him, e.g. Junayd and Shibli and Jurayri and Husri. Some accuse him of magic and matters coming under that head, but in our days the Grand Shaykh Abu Sa'id b. Abu 'l-Khayr and Shaykh Abu 'l-Qasim Gurgani and Shaykh Abu 'l- Abbas Shaqani looked upon him with favour, and in their eyes he was a great man. The Master Abu 'l-Qasim Qushayri remarks that if al-Hallaj was a genuine spiritualist he is not to be banned on the ground of popular condemnation, and if he was banned by Sufism and rejected by the Truth he is not to be approved on the ground of popular approval. Therefore we leave him to the judgment of God, and honour him according to the tokens of the Truth which we have found him to possess. But of all these Shaykhs only a few deny the perfection of his merit and the purity of his spiritual state and the abundance of his ascetic practices. It would be an act of dishonesty to omit his biography from this book. Some persons pronounce his outward behaviour to be that of an infidel, and disbelieve in him and charge him with trickery and magic, and suppose that Husayn b. Mansur

Hallaj is that heretic of Baghdad who was the master of Muhammad b. Zakariyya and the companion of Abu Sa'id the Carmathian; but this Husayn whose character is in dispute was a Persian and a native of Bayda (near Shiraz), and his rejection by the Shaykhs was due, not to any attack on religion and doctrine, but to his conduct and behaviour. At first he was a pupil of Sahl b. 'Abdallah, whom he left, without asking permission, in order to attach himself to Amr b. Uthman Makki. Then he left Amr b. Uthman, again without asking permission, and sought to associate with Junayd, but Junayd would not receive him. This is the reason why he is banned by all the Shaykhs. Now, one who is banned on account of his conduct is not banned on account of his principles. Do you not see that Shibli said: 'Al-Hallaj and I are of one belief, but my madness saved me, while his intelligence destroyed him?' Had his religion been suspected, Shibli would not have said: 'Al-Hallaj and I are of one belief.' And Muhammad b. Khafif said: 'He is a divinely learned man' (alim-i rabbani). Al-Hallaj is the author of brilliant compositions and allegories and polished sayings in theology and jurisprudence. I have seen fifty works by him at Baghdad and in the neighbouring districts, and some in Khuzistan and Fars and Khurasan. All his sayings are like the first visions of novices; some of them are stronger, some weaker, some easier, some more unseemly than others. When God bestows a vision on anyone, and he endeavours to describe what he has seen with the power of ecstasy and the help of Divine grace, his words are obscure, especially if he expresses himself with haste and self-admiration: then they are more repugnant to the imaginations, and incomprehensible to the minds, of those who hear them, and then people say, 'This is a sublime utterance,' either believing it or not, but equally ignorant of its meaning whether they believe or deny. On the other hand, when persons of true spirituality and insight have visions, they make no effort to describe them, and do not occupy themselves with self-admiration on that account, and are careless of praise and blame alike, and are undisturbed by denial and belief.

It is absurd to charge al-Hallaj with being a magician. According to the principles of Muhammadan orthodoxy, magic is real, just as miracles are real; but the manifestation of magic in the state of perfection is infidelity, whereas the manifestation of miracles in the state of perfection is knowledge of God (ma'rifat), because the former is the result of God's anger, while the latter is the corollary of His being well pleased. I will explain this more fully in the chapter on the affirmation of miracles. By consent of all Sunnites who are endowed with perspicacity, no Moslem can be a magician and no infidel can be held in honour, for contraries never meet. Husayn, as long as he lived, wore the garb of piety, consisting in prayer and praise of God and continual fasts and fine sayings on the subject of Unification. If his actions were magic, all this could not possibly have proceeded from him. Consequently, they must have been miracles, and miracles are vouchsafed only to a true saint. Some orthodox theologians reject him on the ground that his sayings are pantheistic *(ba-ma'ni-yi imtizaj u ittihad)*, but the offence lies solely in the expression, not in the meaning. A person overcome with rapture has not the power of expressing himself correctly; besides, the meaning of the expression may be difficult to apprehend, so that people mistake the writer's intention, and repudiate, not his real meaning, but a notion which they have formed for themselves. I have seen at Baghdad and in the adjoining districts a number of heretics who pretend to be the followers of al-Hallaj and make his sayings an argument for their heresy *(zandaqa)* and call themselves Hallajis. They spoke of him in the same terms of exaggeration *(ghuluww)* as the Rafidis (Shi'ites) apply to 'Ali. I will refute their doctrines in the chapter concerning the different Sufi sects. In conclusion, you must know that the sayings of al-Hallaj should not be taken as a model, inasmuch as he was an ecstatic *(maghlub andar hal-i khud)*, not firmly settled *(mutamakkin)* and a man needs to be firmly settled before his sayings can be considered authoritative. Therefore, although he is dear to my heart, yet his 'path' is not soundly established on any principle, and his state is not fixed in any position, and his experiences are largely mingled with error. When my own visions began I derived much support from him, that is to say, in the way of evidences *(barahin)*. At an earlier time I composed a book in explanation of his sayings and demonstrated their sublimity by proofs and arguments. Furthermore, in another work, entitled *Minhaj*, I have spoken of his life from beginning to end; and now I have given some account of him in this place. How can a doctrine whose principles require to be corroborated with so much caution be followed and imitated? Truth and idle fancy never agree. He is continually seeking to fasten upon some erroneous theory. It is related that he said: *Al-alsinat mustantiqdt tahta nutqiha mustahlikat,* i.e. 'speaking tongues are the destruction of silent hearts'. Such expressions are entirely mischievous. Expression of the meaning of reality is futile. If the meaning exists it is not lost by expression, and if it is non-existent it is not created by expression."

SELECTED BIBLIOGRAPHY

Divan al-Hallaj: Kamil M. Shaibi, Baghdad, 1974.

Mansur Hallaj: The Tawasin, Translation & Introduction by Paul Smith, New Humanity Books, Campbells Creek, 2013.

The Passion of al-Hallaj by Louis Massignon, 4 vols, Trans. by Herbert Mason, Princeton University Press 1983.

Hallaj: Mystic and Martyr, by Louis Massignon, Translated, edited abridged by Herbert Mason. Princeton University Press. 1994.

Al-Hallaj. Herbert W. Mason. Curzon Press, Surrey, 1995.

The Tawasin of Mansur al-Hallaj, Translated by Aisha Abd Ar-Rahman At-Tarumana, Diwan Press, Berkeley, 1974.

Sufi Poems, A Mediaeval Anthology by Martin Lings, Islamic Texts Society, Cambridge, 2004. (Pages 26-41).

A Critical Appreciation of Arabic Mystical Poetry by Dr. S.H. Nadeem, Adam Pub. New Delhi, 2003. (Pages 53-71.)

Islamic Mystical Poetry: Sufi Verse from the Early Mystics to Rumi, Edited with translations and introduction by Mahmood Jamal, Penguin Books, London. (Pages 13-34).

The Way of the Mystics: The Early Christian Mystics and the Rise of the Sufis by Margaret Smith... reprint Sheldon Press 1976.

Hallaj: Poemes mystiques, Trans. etc., Sami-Ali, Sindbad, Arles, 1985.

Muslim Saints and Mystics... Episodes from the Tadhkirat al-Auliya' (The Lives of the Saints) by Farid al-Din 'Attar Translated by A.J. Arberry. Routledge & Kegan Paul 1966. (Pages 264-272).

Kashf Al-Mahjub of Al-Hujwiri: The Oldest Persian Treatise on Sufism By 'Ali B. 'Uthman Al-Jullani Al-Hujwiri, Translated by Reynold A. Nicholson, Luzac & Co. London 1911. (Pages 50-53 et al).

Reorientations/Arabic and Persian Poetry Edited by Suzanne Pinckney Stetkevych, Indiana University Press, 1994. (Pages 93-94).

The Idea of Personality in Sufism by Reynold Alleyne Nicholson, Cambridge, 1923 (Pages 27-37).

The Death of al-Hallaj: A Dramatic Narrative by Herbert Mason, University of Notre Dame Press, 1979.

The Tawasin of Mansur al-Hallaj: Interpreted in Poetry by Jabez L. Van Cleef, Spirit Son Text, New Jersey, 2008. (In masnavi form).

The Perfect Master *(Qutub).*

Mansur al-Hallaj is considered by many of the greatest poets and Masters of Sufism to have been a God-realized soul, a Perfect Master *(Qutub)*. I will now try to define God-realization and the clearest and best definition that I know is that by Meher Baba in *Discourses* Sufism Reoriented, San Francisco 6th Edition 1967: "To arrive at true self-knowledge is to arrive at God-realisation. God-realisation is a unique state of consciousness. It is different from all the other states of consciousness because all the other states of consciousness are experienced through the medium of the individual mind; whereas the state of God-consciousness is in no way dependent upon the individual mind or any other medium. A medium is necessary for knowing something other than one's own self. For knowing one's own self no medium is necessary. In fact, the association of consciousness with the mind is definitely a hindrance rather than a help for the attainment of realisation. The individual mind is the seat of the ego or the consciousness of being isolated. It creates the limited individuality, which at once feeds on and is fed by the illusion of duality, time and change. So, in order to know the Self as it is, consciousness has to be completely freed from the limitation of the individual mind. In other words, the individual mind has to disappear but consciousness has to be retained... The consciousness which was hitherto associated with the individual mind is now freed and untrammeled and brought into direct contact and unity with the Ultimate Reality. Since there is now no veil between consciousness and the Ultimate Reality, consciousness is fused with the Absolute and eternally abides in It as an inseparable aspect promoting an unending state of infinite knowledge and unlimited bliss...

"God-realisation is a personal state of consciousness belonging to the soul which has transcended the domain of the mind. Other souls continue to remain in bondage and though they also are bound to receive God-realisation one day they can only attain it by freeing their consciousness from the burden of the ego and the limitations of the individual mind. Hence the attainment of God-realisation has a direct significance only for the soul which has emerged out of the time-process . . . It is possible for an aspirant to rise up to the mental sphere of existence through his own unaided efforts, but dropping the mental body amounts to the surrenderance of individual existence: This last and all-important step cannot be taken except through the help of a Perfect Master who is himself God-realised."

R.A. Nicholson in Chapter two, being an essay on the book of the Sufi Master 'Abdu 'l-Karim ibn Ibrahim al-Jili (born in 1365)… not to be confused with another famous Perfect Master Gilani born 200 years earlier… 'The Perfect Man' *(Insanu 'l-kamil)* of his *Studies in Islamic Mysticism* Cambridge University Press 1921 in which his translation states:

"What do Sufis mean when they speak of the Perfect Man *(al-insanu 'l-kamil)*, a phrase which seems first to have been used by the celebrated Ibnu 'l-'Arabi, although the notion underlying it is almost as old as Sufism itself? The question might be answered in different ways, but if we seek a general definition, perhaps we may describe the Perfect Man as a man who has fully realised his essential oneness with the Divine Being in whose likeness he is made. This experience, enjoyed by prophets and saints and shadowed forth in symbols to others, is the foundation of the Sufi theosophy. Therefore, the class of Perfect Men comprises not only the prophets from Adam to Mohammed, but also the superlatively elect *(khususu 'l-khusus)* amongst the Sufis, i.e., the persons named collectively *awliya,* plural of *wali,* a word originally meaning "near," which is used for "friend," *"protége,"* or "devotee." Since the *wali* or saint is the popular type of Perfect Man, it should be understood that the essence of Mohammedan saintship, as of prophecy, is nothing less than Divine illumination, immediate vision and knowledge of things unseen and unknown, when the veil of sense is suddenly lifted and the conscious self passes away in the overwhelming glory of "the One true Light." An ecstatic feeling of oneness with God constitutes the *wali*. It is the end of the Path *(tariqa)* in so far as the discipline of the Path is meant to predispose and prepare the disciple to receive this incalculable gift of Divine grace, which is not gained or lost by anything that a man may do, but comes to him in proportion to the measure and degree of spiritual capacity with which he was created.

"Two special functions of the *wali* further illustrate the relation of the popular saint-cult to mystical philosophy—(1) his function as a mediator, (2) his function as a cosmic power. The Perfect Man, as will be explained in the course of our argument, unites the One and the Many, so that the universe depends on him for its continued existence. In Mohammedan religious life the *wali* occupies the same middle position: he bridges the chasm which the Koran and scholasticism have set between man and an absolutely transcendent God. He brings relief to the distressed, health to the sick, children to the childless, food to the famished, spiritual guidance to those who entrust their souls to his care, blessing to all who visit his tomb and invoke Allah in his name. The walls, from the highest to the lowest, are arranged in a graduated hierarchy, with the *Qutub* at their head, forming "a saintly board of administration by which the invisible government of the world is carried on." Speaking of the *Awtad*—four saints whose rank is little inferior to that of the *Qutub* himself- Hujwiri (*Kashaf al-Mahjub* of Al-Hujwiri, R.A. Nicholson translation Luzac & Co, London 1911, page 228) says: 'It is their office to go round the whole world every night, and if there be any place on which their eyes have not fallen, next day some flaw will appear in that place; and they must then inform the *Qutub*, in order that he may direct his attention to the weak spot, and that by his blessing the imperfection may be remedied.'

"Such experiences and beliefs were partly the cause and partly the consequence of speculation concerning the nature of God and man, speculation which drifted far away from Koranic monotheism into pantheistic and monistic philosophies. The Sufi reciting the Koran in ecstatic prayer and seeming to hear, in the words which he intoned, not his own voice but the voice of God speaking through him, could no longer acquiesce in the orthodox conception of Allah as a Being utterly different from all other beings. This dogma was supplanted by faith in a

Divine Reality *(al-Haqq)*, a God who is the creative principle and ultimate ground of all that exists. While Sufis, like Moslems in general, affirm the transcendence of God and reject the notion of infusion or incarnation *(hulul)*, it is an interesting fact that one of the first attempts in Islam to indicate more precisely the meaning of mystical union was founded on the Christian doctrine of two natures in God. Hallaj, who dared to say *Ana 'l-Haqq,* 'I am the *Haqq,'* thereby announced that the saint in his deification "becomes the living and personal witness of God." The Jewish tradition that God created Adam in His own image reappeared as a *hadith* (saying of the Prophet) and was put to strange uses by Mohammedan theosophists. Even the orthodox Ghazali hints that here is the key of a great mystery which nothing will induce him to divulge. According to Hallaj, the essence of God's essence is Love. Before the creation God loved Himself in absolute unity and through love revealed Himself to Himself alone. Then, desiring to behold that love-in-aloneness, that love without otherness and duality, as an external object, He brought forth from non-existence an image of Himself, endowed with all His attributes and names. This Divine image is Adam, in and by whom God is made manifest-- divinity objectified in humanity. Hallaj, however, distinguishes the human nature *(nasut)* from the Divine *(lahut)*. Though mystically united, they are not essentially identical and interchangeable. Personality survives even in union: water does not become wine, though wine be mixed with it. Using a more congenial metaphor, Hallaj says in verses which are often quoted:

I'm the One I love, the One I love is me,
we are two spirits that live... in one body.
If you see me, then... you see that One,
and, if you see that One... both, you see.
(Trans. of poem by Paul Smith)

"...Jili belongs to the school of Sufis who hold that Being is one, that all apparent differences are modes, aspects and manifestations of reality, that the phenomenal is the outward expression of the real. He begins by defining essence as that to which names and attributes are referred; it may be either existent or non-existent, *i.e.,* existing only in name, like the fabulous bird called 'Anqa. Essence that really exists is of two kinds: Pure Being, or God, and Being joined to not-being, *i.e.,* the world of created things. The essence of God is unknowable *per se;* we must seek knowledge of it through its names and attributes. It is a substance with two accidents, eternity and everlastingness; with two qualities, creativeness and creatureliness; with two descriptions, uncreatedness and origination in time; with two names, Lord and slave (God and man); with two aspects, the outward or visible, which is the present world, and the inward or invisible, which is the world to come; both necessity and contingency are predicated of it, and it may be regarded either as non-existent for itself but existent for other, or as non-existent for other but existent for itself.

"Pure Being, as such, has neither name nor attribute; only when it gradually descends from its absoluteness and enters the realm of manifestation, do names and attributes appear imprinted on it. The sum, of these attributes is the universe, which is 'phenomenal' only in the sense that it shows reality under the form of externality. Although, from this standpoint, the distinction of essence and attribute must be admitted, the two are ultimately one, like water and ice. The so-called phenomenal world—the world of attributes—is no illusion: it really exists as the self-revelation or other self of the Absolute. In denying any real difference between essence and attribute, Jili makes Being identical with Thought. The world expresses God's idea of Himself, or as Ibnu 'l-'Arabi puts it, 'we ourselves are the attributes by which we describe God; our existence is merely an objectification of His existence. God is necessary to us in order that we may exist, while we are necessary to Him in order that He may be manifested to Himself.'

"Jili calls the simple essence, apart from all qualities and relations, 'the dark mist' *(al-'Ama)*. It develops consciousness by passing through three stages of manifestation, which modify its simplicity. The first stage is Oneness *(Ahadiyya)*, the second is He-ness *(Huwiyya)*, and the third is I-ness *(Aniyya)*. By this process of descent Absolute Being has become the subject and object of all thought and has revealed itself as Divinity with distinctive attributes embracing the whole series of existence. The created world is the outward aspect of that which in its inward aspect is God. Thus in the Absolute we find a principle of diversity, which it evolves by moving downwards, so to speak, from a plane beyond quality and relation, beyond even the barest unity, until by degrees it clothes itself with manifold names and attributes and takes visible shape in the infinite variety of Nature. But 'the One remains, the Many change and pass.' The Absolute cannot rest in diversity. Opposites must be reconciled and at last united, the Many must again be One. Recurring to Jili's metaphor, we may say that as water becomes ice and then water once more, so the Essence crystallised in the world of attributes seeks to return to its pure and simple self. And in order to do so, it must move upwards, reversing the direction of its previous descent from absoluteness. We have seen how reality, without ceasing to be reality, presents itself in the form of appearance: by what means, then, does appearance cease to be appearance and disappear in the abysmal darkness of reality?

"Man, in virtue of his essence, is the cosmic Thought assuming flesh and connecting Absolute Being with the world of Nature.

"While every appearance shows some attribute of reality, Man is the microcosm in which all attributes are united, and in him alone does the Absolute become conscious of itself in all its diverse aspects. To put it in another way, the Absolute, having completely realised itself in human nature, returns into itself through the medium of human nature; or, more intimately, God and man become one in the Perfect Man—the enraptured prophet or saint—whose religious function as a mediator between man and God corresponds with his metaphysical function as the unifying principle by means of which the opposed terms of reality and appearance are harmonised. Hence the upward movement of the Absolute from the sphere of manifestation back to the unmanifested

Essence takes place in and through the unitive experience of the soul; and so we have exchanged philosophy for mysticism.

"Jili distinguishes three phases of mystical illumination or revelation *(tajalli)*, which run parallel, as it were, to the three stages—Oneness, He-ness, and I-ness—traversed by the Absolute in its descent to consciousness.

"In the first phase, called the Illumination of the Names, the Perfect Man receives the mystery that is conveyed by each of the names of God, and he becomes one with the name in such sort that he answers the prayer of any person who invokes God by the name in question.

"Similarly, in the second phase he receives the Illumination of the Attributes and becomes one with them, *i.e.,* with the Divine Essence as qualified by its various attributes: life, knowledge, power, will, and so forth. For example, God reveals Himself to some mystics through the attribute of life. Such a man, says Jili, is the life of, the whole universe; he feels that his life permeates all things sensible and ideal, that all words, deeds, bodies, and spirits derive their existence from him. If he be endued with the attribute of knowledge, he knows the entire content of past, present, and future existence, how everything came to be or is coming or will come to be, and why the non-existent does not exist: all this he knows both synthetically and analytically. The Divine attributes are classified by the author under four heads: (1) attributes of the Essence, (2) attributes of Beauty, (3) attributes of Majesty, (4) attributes of Perfection. He says that all created things are mirrors in which Absolute Beauty is reflected. What is ugly has its due place in the order of existence no less than what is beautiful, and equally belongs to the Divine perfection: evil, therefore, is only relative. As was stated above, the Perfect Man reflects all the Divine attributes, including even the Essential ones, such as unity and eternity, which he shares with no other being in this world or the next.

"The third and last phase is the Illumination of the Essence. Here the Perfect Man becomes *absolutely* perfect. Every attribute has vanished, the Absolute has returned into itself.

"In the theory thus outlined we can recognise a monistic form of the myth which represents the Primal Man, the first-born of God, as sinking into matter, working there as a creative principle, longing for deliverance, and, at last finding the way back to his source. Jili calls the Perfect Man the preserver of the universe, the *Qutb* or Pole on which all the spheres of existence revolve. He is the final cause of creation, *i.e.*, the means by which God sees Himself, for the Divine names and attributes cannot be seen, as a whole, except in the Perfect Man. He is a copy made in the image of God; therefore in him is that which corresponds to the Essence with its two correlated aspects of He-ness and I-ness, *i.e.*, inwardness and outwardness, or divinity and humanity. His real nature is threefold, as Jili expressly declares in the following verses, which no one can read without wondering how a Moslem could have written them:

If you say that it (the Essence) is One, you are right;
or if you say that it is Two, it is in fact Two.
Or if you say, 'No, it is Three,' you are right,
for that is the real nature of Man."
(End of Nicholson quote)

The Tomb of Hallaj in Karkh.

'Anal-Haqq' or 'I am the Truth' of Hallaj.

In his book of 'lectures' *The Idea of Personality in Sufism* the great translator of Rumi's work and other Sufi poets R.A. Nicholson states... "The words *Ana 'l-Haqq* occur in an extraordinary book composed by Hallaj, the *Kitab al-Tawasin,* which was edited in 1913 by M. Louis Massignon. Written in rhymed Arabic prose and divided into eleven brief sections, it sets forth a doctrine of saintship—a doctrine founded on personal experience and clothed in the form of a subtle yet passionate dialectic. The style is so technical and obscure that even with the help of the Persian commentary we can sometimes only guess what meaning the writer intended to convey. Instead of translating the text, the editor has devoted years of patient labour to understanding and illustrating it, with the result that his monograph on Hallaj must be studied carefully by everyone interested in Sufism. For it is now clear that the words *Ana I'-Haqq* were not the ejaculation of visionary enthusiasm but the intuitive formula in which a whole system of mystical theology summed itself up. And this system is not only the first in time, it is also profoundly original. The power and vitality of this man's ideas are attested by the influence which they asserted upon his successors. His ashes were scattered, swept away, as he prophesied, by rushing winds and running waters, but his words lived after him and we see them, all through the Middle Ages, rising like sparks and kindling to new life.

I cannot attempt to give you a full account of the doctrines contained in the *Tasawin* and supplemented by numerous fragments which Massignon has collected. We may begin by asking, "What did Hallaj mean when he said *Ana 'l-Haqq?*" The expression *al-Haqq* is commonly used by Sufis to denote the Creator as opposed to *al-khalq,* "the creatures," and there is no doubt that it bears this signification here: *Ana 'l-Haqq,* "I am the Creative Truth," as Massignon renders it (*Tawasin,* p.175).

"Hallaj," he says, "while affirming the transcendence of the idea of God, did not at all conceive it as being inaccessible to man. From the old Jewish and Christian tradition that God created man in His own image Hallaj deduced a doctrine of creation, which had its counterpart in a doctrine of deification: the deified man finds in himself, by means of 9a mystical) asceticism, the reality of the Divine image which God has imprinted on him. We possess several Hallajian fragments that leave no doubt as to this. In the longest, Hallaj explains the matter thus: Before all things, before the creation, before

His knowledge of the creation, God in His unity was holding an ineffable discourse with Himself and contemplating the splendour of His essence in itself. That pure simplicity of His self-admiration is Love, which in His essence is the essence of the essence, beyond all limitation of attributes. In His perfect isolation God loves Himself, praises Himself, and manifests Himself by Love. And it was this first manifestation of Love in the Divine Absolute that determined the multiplicity of His attributes and His names. Then God, by His essence, in His essence, desired to project out of Himself his supreme joy, that Love in its aloneness, that He might behold it and speak to it. He looked in eternity and brought forth from non-existence and image, an image of Himself, endowed with all His attributes and all His names: Adam. The Divine look made that form to be His image unto everlasting. God saluted it, glorified it, chose it, and inasmuch as He manifested Himself by it and in it, that created form became *Huwa Huwa,* I Ie, I Ie!" (*Tawasin* page 129).

The first of the following verses by Hallaj refers to Adam, the second is said to refer to Jesus:

Glory to God Who revealed in His humanity the secret of His radiant divinity.

And then appeared to His creatures visibly in the shape of one who eats and drinks. [Tawasin p. 130]

Here you will notice, we have the doctrine of two natures in God—a divine nature *[lahut]* and a human nature *[nasut]*. These terms are borrowed by Syrian Christianity, which uses them to denote the two natures of Christ. Further, Hallaj in describing the union of the *lahut* with the *nasut*—or, as he generally says, of the Divine Spirit with the human spirit—employs the term *hulul;* and *hulul* is a word associated, in Muslim minds, with the Christian doctrine of the Incarnation. In his poems his own spirit and the Divine Spirit appear as lovers conversing with each other and most intimately united.

Thy Spirit is mingled in my spirit even as wine is mingled in pure water.

When everything touches Thee, it touches me. Lo, in every case Thou art I. [Tawasin p.134]

And again:

I am He whom I love, and He whom I love is I,

We are two spirits dwelling in one body.

If thou seest me, thou seest Him.

And if thou seest Him, thou seest us both.

[Tawasin p. 134]

While Hallaj asserts the pre-existence of Mohammad as the Light from which all prophecy emanates, it is not Mohammad but Jesus in whom he finds the perfect type of the ''deified man', whose personality is not destroyed but transfigured and essentialised, so that he stands forth as the personal witness and representative of God, revealing from within himself *al-Haqq*, the Creator through whom he exists, the Creative Truth in whom he has all his being. (*Tawasin* pp 162, 175.) End of quote of Nicholson.

In his great *masnavi* poem that has become a famous manual of Sufism 'The Rose Garden of Mysteries' the Sufi Master Poet Shabistari (1250-1320) commenting on this saying of Hallaj poses the following question...

QUESTION

'I am The Truth!' When, to reveal this is appropriate?
Why call that one a babbler... vain imposter, incarnate?

ANSWER

'I am The Truth' is a revelation of absolute mystery,
and... except for 'The Truth' who revealing it can be?
All of the atoms of the world, all of those like Mansur,
one could think to be drunk and heavy with wine, for
they are continually singing this song full of praise...
they in this spiritual truth are spending all their days.
If you desire that its meaning be made clear to you,

then go and be reading the text 'God, all praise You'.
When eventually the 'self' as cotton you have carded,
from you like that 'wool-carder' such will be shouted.
Take out from your ears that cotton of your illusion...
be listening to the call of... 'The Almighty, the One'.
From 'The Truth' this call is always coming to you...
so why are you waiting for the last day... to be true?
Come into the 'valley of peace' because immediately
the bush will be saying to you 'Truly I am God', see?
If 'I am The Truth' for the burning bush was lawful,
why... in mouth of a good man would it be unlawful?
Every one whose heart is purified, without any doubt,
that exists no being but One, knows without a doubt.
To be saying 'I am', only to 'The Truth' is belonging,
for both essence and illusory appearance is not being.
Glory of 'The Truth' does not allow for any duality...
because there is no 'I' or 'We' or 'You' in that Glory!
'I' and 'We' and 'You' and 'He' are all only one thing,
because in Unity there is no distinction of and being.
And so, every person who as a void is of self empty,
in that one is echoing 'I am The Truth'... constantly;
that one is taking his side that is eternal, 'other' dies,
the traveler and travel and traveling... all in One lies.

From the 'other' incarnation, communion are springing,

but... from the spiritual journey the Unity is arriving.

Separated from 'The Truth' is illusionary existence...

'The Truth' is no creature; God, none does experience.

Here... Incarnation and Communion are impossible;

because, duality within unity is obviously impossible.

The existence of creatures and diversity is an illusion,

for not all that seems to be can honestly be relied upon.

(From, 'The Rose Garden of Mysteries' by Shabistari, Translation
& Introduction by Paul Smith, New Humanity Books, Campbells
Creek, 2012.

Four Master Poets of Baghdad who influenced Hallaj.

AL NURI (d.907). Abu 'l-Husayn al-Nuri was a native of Baghdad. He was a friend of al-Junaid who was for a time the Spiritual Master of Hallaj. He was a leading figure of Sufism in the region. His name 'Nuri' means 'Man of Light.'

Al-Nuri was devout and had an ascetic temperament. It is said that when he left for work in the morning, he would buy a few loaves of bread and then distribute them to the poor on his walk. He would then go to the mosque and pray until noon before arriving at work... never having eaten food for himself.

But even with his compassion and his striving, at a certain point he became frustrated that he was still buffeted with desires and hadn't penetrated to inner mystical truth. He then made a firm resolve to follow God's will in everything and not to be distracted by comforts and desires. He was determined to confront every aspect of himself, even considering the possibility that his past striving and good works had been hypocritical... a determination to remove all falsity and barriers between himself and God.

In this process, he began to recognize that the carnal mind, the grasping, false self, claimed a portion of everything the heart touched. Thus, when God sent him divine insight, this grasping identity stole a portion of it... which explained the poverty of his mystical experience to that point. From that point on, he thwarted the false self at every turn. Even in service to others, if he found the carnal mind gaining satisfaction, he quickly stopped and sought new ways to help others. Al-Nuri said that through doing this he slowly discovered the way to true mystical insight.

Further Reading...

Anthology of Classical Arabic Poetry, Translation & Introduction by Paul Smith, New Humanity Books, Campbells Creek, 2009.
Sufi Poems, A Medieval Anthology by Martin Lings, Islamic Texts Society, Cambridge, 2004. (Pages 16-19).
A Critical Appreciation of Arabic Mystical Poetry by Dr. S.H. Nadeem, Adam Publishers. New Delhi, 2003.
The Way of the Mystics: The Early Christian Mystics and the Rise of the Sufis by Margaret Smith... reprint Sheldon Press 1976.
In the Garden of Myrtles: Studies in Early Islamic Mysticism by Tor Andrae, Translated by Birgitta Sharpe. State University of New York Press, Albany. 1987.
Muslim Saints and Mystics... Episodes from the Tadhkirat al-Auliya' (The Lives of the Saints) by Farid al-Din 'Attar Translated by A.J. Arberry. Routledge & Kegan Paul 1966. (Pages 221-231.)

Some examples of his poetry...

Qit'as...

"Don't tell," You said, then… into mysteries beyond any speech

You took my questioning soul: can any words describe the indescribable?

Not each one who cries, "Look, I am this," one takes his word:

when deeds show one is so then You him as Your own find claimable.

Through concentration, 'I' would go, a path to You, I'd set:
but, none may come to You, except, as You want them to.
Lord I can't without You, but Your hand stops me leaving:
some desired to come to You… this hope You created, too;
see, I've cut off all thought… killed me, so I'm only Yours:
heart's Beloved, how long? With separation… I'm through.

"For tomorrow's festival," they cried, "what robe will you wear?"

I replied: "Robe He gave, Who poured me many a bitter potion:

poverty, patience cover a heart seeing at every feast its Lover…

can there be finer garb to greet Friend than one He lends to one?

When You aren't near, each moment is an age of grief, and fear:

if I see and hear You, days are joyful, life's a festival in the sun!"

God, I fear You: not because I dread any wrath to come:

how can one fear… You are the best Friend, obviously?

You know my heart's design, the mind's secret purpose:

I adore You, Divine Light, a lesser light would blind me.

Lord, I thank You… not that I can repay Your love by my thanking:

so, it may be said about me, "He, took God's bounties, gratefully."

All glorious hours I spent with You, have now become my memories:

gratitude's last treasure… joys of pleasures remembered, fully.

"Today I'll reach my goal!" I cried, but the goal's so far:

I fight, fail; yet, to have tried and lost, that itself is war.

Now, hope's lost, but, Your love will forgive and Your compassion approve or heaven's lost, and I will wander far.

I'm veiled from Time and my veil's my feeling for Him: this wonder in me for His Infinite value... more than I! Time cannot see that I have slipped through its hands... and I do not see Time's works anymore, or how they fly, because I am now only awake to be fulfilling His order, and the rest of my life for Time why should I care... why?

My love overflows such that I'd remember Him forever; and yet my remembering, that'd be amazing to explain, has become ecstasy; and it is amazing that even ecstasy from any memory of near and far, has vanished... again!

*

JUNAID (830-910). Junaid ibn Muhammad Abu al-Qasim al-Khazzaz al-Baghdadi was one of the great early Sufis.

He laid the groundwork for *sober* mysticism in contrast to that of *God-intoxicated* Sufis like Bayazid Bistami, Mansur Hallaj and Abu Said. In the process of the trial of Hallaj his former disciple, the caliph of the time demanded his death and he issued this: "From the outward appearance he is to die and we judge according to the outward appearance and God knows better."

Further Reading...

The Life, Personality and Writings of Al-Junayd. Edited and Translated by Dr. Ali Hassan Abdel-Kader, Luzac, 1978.
A Critical Appreciation of Arabic Mystical Poetry by Dr. S.H. Nadeem, Adam Publishers. New Delhi, 2003.
The Way of the Mystics: The Early Christian Mystics and the Rise of the Sufis by Margaret Smith... reprint Sheldon Press 1976.
In the Garden of Myrtles: Studies in Early Islamic Mysticism by Tor Andrae, Translated by Birgitta Sharpe. State University of New York Press, Albany. 1987.
Muslim Saints and Mystics... Episodes from the Tadhkirat al-Auliya' (The Lives of the Saints) by Farid al-Din 'Attar Translated by A.J. Arberry. Routledge & Kegan Paul 1966. (pages 192-214.)
Anthology of Classical Arabic Poetry, Translation & Introduction by Paul Smith, New Humanity Books, Campbells Creek, 2009.

Some examples of his poetry...

Qit'as...

Over their hearts flew His desire and they arrived

in the neighbourhood of that perfect, glorified One.

Under His glory's shadow they are close to Him,

there where their souls are stirring under His Sun.

They're going there to discover honour and insight

and they're returning with every kind of perfection.

They march with the unique glory of that One's

attributes and they're trailing robes of Unification.
And what happens next is far beyond any way of
describing, so, it is best let it stay a secret, my son.

You, burner of my heart's fire with Your omnipotence,
if You'd wanted You'd have put it out with... Yourself.
If I should die from fear and worry, I won't be blamed
for what You've done to me: it is not because of myself.

O Lord, now I've known what's inside my heart:
secretly, with my Beloved I've held conversation.
And so, in a fashion, we are One, we are united,
but our condition in another is one of separation.
Although awe has hidden You from my glances,
ecstasy brought You into my innermost location.

O God, my God, if You should happen to turn
cold on me... and turn Your face from me away,
my soul could never escape its longing for You,
even if this life it will leave behind... give away.

SUMNUN (d. 915). Abu'l-Hasan Sumnun ibn Mamzah al-Basri was from Baghdad and like al-Nuri was a friend of Junaid. He was called *al-Muhibb,* the Lover.

Further Reading…

Sufi Poems, A Medieval Anthology by Martin Lings, Islamic Texts Society, Cambridge, 2004. (Pages 21-25).
Muslim Saints and Mystics… Episodes from the Tadhkirat al-Auliya' (The Lives of the Saints) by Farid al-Din 'Attar Translated by A.J. Arberry. Routledge & Kegan Paul 1966. (Pages 239-243.)
Anthology of Classical Arabic Poetry, Translation & Introduction by Paul Smith, New Humanity Books, Campbells Creek, 2009.

Some of his poetry…

Qit'as…

I'm longing at every dawn and as night is falling,
and I answer that one when love calls at night…
as day disappears my love is growing stronger,
although that time of love is now lost from sight.

Inside of me I felt empty, until I discovered Your love:
on life, things, I'd muse slightly, but usually playing;
then, when my heart was called by Your love, it went,
and now lost to me forever, it's in Your court, staying.

If I'm lying may separation from You be my payment,
if in the world any joy in other than You I am finding,
and if anything should seem lovely to me in any land, if
to these two eyes of mine... You they're not seeing!
And so, if it's Your will, then bring me to You, or not:
whatever happens, but my heart only You, is wanting!

There's no doubt in my heart You're the Beloved:
it would no longer live again, if this soul lost You.
You made me thirst for Union that You can give
if in You I rested, if "O my thirst!" I cried to You.

Existence of the seer is obliterated by What is seen:
existence is obliterated by It, so it's without meaning.
You tossed me into Your Divinity's ocean, to swim,
where I don't exist but from in You, You I'm desiring.

If once my eye wept or kept watch for other than You,
let it never receive that Gift... that it was longing for!
If it on purpose looked on other than You may it never
graze Faith's meadow, or see Your fair face, anymore.

SHIBLI (861-946). A pupil and disciple of Junaid of Baghdad and one who had met and was a friend of... Mansur Hallaj, Shibli is one of the famous Sufis. He was originally from Khurasan. In the book *Rawdat al-jannat,* and in other biographies, many mystical poems and sayings have been recorded of him. Ansari has said: "The first person to speak in symbols was Dhu al-Nun of Egypt. Then came Junaid and he systematized this science, extended it, and wrote books on it. Shibli, in his turn, took it to the pulpit." He died in 946 at the age of 87. He composed his poems in Arabic.

Further Reading...

A Critical Appreciation of Arabic Mystical Poetry by Dr. S.H. Nadeem, Adam Publishers. New Delhi, 2003.
Sufi Poems, A Mediaeval Anthology by Martin Lings, Islamic Texts Society, Cambridge, 2004 (Pages 41-7).
The Way of the Mystics: The Early Christian Mystics and the Rise of the Sufis by Margaret Smith... reprint Sheldon Press 1976.
Muslim Saints and Mystics... Episodes from the Tadhkirat al-'Auliya' (The Lives of the Saints) by Farid al-Din 'Attar Translated by A.J. Arberry. Routledge & Kegan Paul 1966. (Pages 277-287.)
Anthology of Classical Arabic Poetry, Translation & Introduction by Paul Smith, New Humanity Books, Campbells Creek, 2009.

Some of his poems...

Ruba'i...

I will put upon me a fine robe of patience...
keeping awake at night for longer makes sense.
I am not yet willing to be patient completely...
a bit at a time soul I'll try bring, to my defense.

Qit'as...

The science of the Sufis has no bound,
a science, high, celestial and divine...
in it, hearts of Masters' plunged deep;
men of wisdom know them by that sign.

Majnun declared his love, while I concealed
my passion... so I attained ecstasy's state.
On the Day of Judgement, when lovers are
called to come up... only I will as a lover rate!

A friend asked, "How's Your patience with them?"
I replied, "Does patience exist? I need to be asked?"
The heat of love in my heart is more fierce than fire,
more sweet than piety...sharper than a knife whetted.

I mentioned You, not because I'd forgotten You, even
momentarily… to remember with the tongue is easier.
From ecstasy I'd almost died… such was my longing,
and I was so anxious my heart kept beating… faster!
Then, when the ecstasy revealed to me You were here
before me… I then did see Your presence, everywhere!
So I communicated with the Existence without words
and saw One I knew, without having to at One stare.

A shadow of a cloud from You one day was over us,
with lightning it dazed us, but no rain was coming:
darkness didn't clear and so despairing were many,
no downpour arrived for the thirsting to be drinking.

Glancing my way He let me see how much He cared:
I was aflame, it melted my heart, as He moved away.
He isn't *not* here, as consolation I can remember Him,
and He never *really* left… and now 'I' might go away!

This case of mine is strange, I'm unique in this state:
among mankind I'm the only one: none, is beyond me!
I am eternally in Your form and 'me', You obliterated:
so, I am not now of created beings… in fact, I'm Free!

53

Don't let any moons set or stay bright as our Moon is
full and seeing it full moons bow low because its light
for us is shining brightly day and night… and it's true
that it can not be dulled or changed by time… or might!

Surely you'll have heard that I was staying
in saints' brotherhood, under poets' cupola?
Truth was, I was afraid of being with both,
so with poetry and song I acted like another
with crazy acts of joy or agony and allowed
myself to be placed in a hospital to recover!
I feared of being alone with One, Beloved…
I feared death, old or young, like some other.
That is why I threw a rose as he was on the
cross performing an ablution in blood there.
Mine were acts of a mad lover, it saved me:
bringing death… his out of his reason were.

Sufis & Dervishes: Their Art and Use of Poetry

It has been said that Adam was the first Sufi and Perfect Master (Qutub) and that he was also the first poet as he named everything and so through his 'Adamic Alphabet' (see the *Hebraic Tongue Restored* listed below) all languages were born and so... all poetry. Two of Arabia's most highly regarded scholars of the poetic form also claim he was the father of the poetic form of the *ghazal*.

Sufism is said by many Masters and authors to have always existed since Adam as the esoteric side of each faith that has begun by an appearance of that original Perfect Master coming back as the Rasool, Prophet, Messiah, Avatar, Buddha, etc., whatever that Divine One is called.

Many Perfect Masters (Qutubs) were poets and many were not. Many came after the appearance of the Prophet Mohammed and many came before him. But, Sufis and Dervishes were called by those names after he passed from this world. The first 'Sufi' is probably Mohammed's son-in-law Hazrat Ali who composed one of the first *ghazals* ever recorded that essentially sums up the meaning of Sufism and Dervishness...

You do not know it, but in you is the remedy;

you cause the sickness, but this you don't see.

You are but a small form... this, you assume:

but you're larger than any universe, in reality.

You are the book that of any fallacies is clear,

in you are all letters spelling out, the mystery.

You are the Being, you're the very Being... It:

you contain That, which contained cannot be!

I have used both the terms 'Sufis' and 'Dervishes' in this book because some of the poets within called themselves not one but the other and criticized the other, for... during the time that they were alive, having become corrupt and following false masters. Hafiz, for instance, always called himself a Dervish and often when mentioning Sufis in his poetry it was usually to criticise them. During his lifetime in Shiraz there was an extremist Sufi Order led by a false master and Shaikh Ali Kolah who sided with various dictators and subjected the people to a very vicious brand of fundamentalism (see my biog. of Hafiz, *Hafiz of Shiraz* 3 vols. for Hafiz's almost lifelong clash with this false Sufi). By the 13th Century many Sufi Orders had become corrupt and full of various dogmas, useless rituals and power hungry and hypocritical shaikhs and false masters. Those who called themselves 'Dervishes' then really meant 'true Sufis'.

The first Sufi and Dervish poets composed in Arabic even though some of them, including the famous and infamous Sufi martyr Mansur Hallaj, were originally from Persia... he was from near Shiraz. From the 10th to the 15th century the vast majority of Sufi and Dervish and other poets in the region composed in Persian, a few in the new languages of Turkish and Urdu and some like Kabir in Hindi; after that... the languages most used by the most conscious and influential poets were Pashtu, Urdu, Punjabi and Sindhi, as the stream of God-consciousness moved originally from Arabia and Egypt to Iraq and Syria then into Iran and Afghanistan and Turkey and finally into the Indian Sub-Continent.

To follow this golden thread of Spiritual Poetry one must follow the true Spiritual Hierarchy of real Saints and God-realized Souls... Perfect Masters, their lives and stories are to be found in the many books listed below and in many others.

What is the essential belief and philosophy of the Sufi and Dervish Masters and Poets? To put it as simply as possibly... The Love of God, the belief in God in human form, the love and respect for all of God's Creation and to try to not hurt anyone or thing. And of course a belief in Truth, Love and

Beauty as the greatest of the Divine Attributes. A belief similar, if not the same as the Christian Mystics and Vedantists and believers in the inner way of most religions.

Hazrat Inayat Khan says in his essay on Sufi Poetry: "There is a saying that a poet is a prophet, and this saying has a great significance and a hidden meaning. There is no doubt that though poetry is not necessarily prophecy, prophecy is born in poetry. If one were to say that poetry is a body which is adopted by the spirit of prophecy, it would not be wrong. Wagner has said that noise is not necessarily music, and the same thing can be said in connection with poetry: that a verse written in rhyme and metre is not necessarily true poetry. Poetry is an art, a music expressed in the beauty and harmony of words. No doubt much of the poetry one reads is meant either as a pastime or for amusement, but real poetry comes from the dancing of the soul. And no one can make the soul dance unless the soul itself is inclined to dance. Also, no soul can dance which is not alive.

In the Bible it is said that no one will enter the kingdom of God whose soul is not born again, and being born means being alive. It is not only a happy disposition or an external inclination to merriment and pleasure that is the sign of a living soul; for external joy and amusement may come simply through the external being of man, although even in this outer joy and happiness there is a glimpse of the inner joy and happiness which is the sign of the soul having been born again. What makes it alive? It makes itself alive when it strikes its depths instead of reaching outward. The soul, after coming up against the iron wall of this life of falsehood, turns back within itself, it encounters itself, and this is how it becomes living.

In order to make this idea more clear I should like to take as an example a man who goes out into the world; a man with thought, with feeling, with energy, with desire, with ambition, with enthusiasm to live and work in life. And because of the actual nature of life, his experience will make him feel constantly up against an iron wall in whatever direction he strikes out. And the nature of man is such that when he meets with an obstacle then he struggles; he lives in the outer life, and he goes on struggling. He does not know any other part of life, for he lives only on the surface. But then there is another man who is sensitive because he has a sympathetic and tender heart, and every blow coming from the outer world, instead of making him want to hit back outwardly, makes him want to strike at himself inwardly. And the consequence of this is that his soul, which after being born on this earth seems to be living but in reality is in a grave, becomes awakened by that action;

and when once the soul is awakened in this way it expresses itself outwardly, whether in music, in art, in poetry, m action, or in whatever way it wishes to express itself.

In this way a poet is born. There are two signs which reveal the poet: one sign is imagination, the other is feeling, and both are essential on the spiritual path. A man, however learned and good, who yet lacks these two qualities, can never arrive at a satisfactory result, especially on the spiritual path.

The sacred scriptures of all ages, whether of the Hindus or the Parsis, the race of Ben Israel or of others, were all given in poetry or in poetic prose. No spiritual person however great, however pious and spiritually advanced, has ever been able to give a scripture to the world unless he was blessed with the gift of poetry. One may ask if this would still be possible nowadays, when sentiment takes second place in life's affairs and people wish everything to be expressed plainly, 'cut and dried' as the saying is, and when one has become so accustomed to having everything, especially in science, explained in clear words. But it must be understood that facts about the names and forms of this world may be scientifically explained in plain words, but when one wishes to interpret the sensation one gets when looking at life, it cannot be explained except m the way that the prophets did in poetry. No one has ever explained nor can anyone ever explain the truth in words. Language exists only for the convenience of everyday affairs; the deepest sentiments cannot be explained in words. The message that the prophets have given to the world at different times is an interpretation in their own words of the idea of life that they have received.

Inspiration begins in poetry and culminates in prophecy. One can picture the poet as a soul which has so to speak risen from its grave and is beginning to make graceful movements; but when the same soul begins to move and to dance in all directions and to touch heaven and earth in its dance, expressing all the beauty it sees -- that is prophecy. The poet when he is developed reads the mind of the universe, although it very often happens that the poet himself does not know the real meaning of what he has said. Very often one finds that a poet has said something, and after many years there comes a moment when he realizes the true meaning of what he said. And this shows that behind all these different activities the divine Spirit is hidden, and the divine Spirit often manifests through an individual without his realizing that it is divine.

In the East the prophet is called *Payghambar,* which means the Messenger, the one who carries somebody's word to someone else. In reality every individual in this world is the medium of an impulse which is hidden behind him, and that impulse he gives out, mostly without knowing it. This is not only so with living beings, but one can see it even in objects; for every object has its purpose, and by fulfilling its purpose that object is fulfilling the scheme of nature. Therefore whatever be the line or activity of a man, whether it is. business or science or music or art or poetry, he is a medium in some way or other. There are mediums of living beings, there are mediums of those who have passed to the other side, and there are mediums that represent their country, their nation, their race. Every individual is acting in his own way as a medium.

When the prophet or the poet dives deep into himself he touches that perfection which is the source and goal of all beings. And as an electric wire connected with a battery receives the force or energy of the battery, so the poet who has touched the innermost depths of his being has touched the perfect God, and from there he derives that wisdom, that beauty, and that power which belong to the perfect Self of God. There is no doubt that in all things there is the real and the false and there is the raw and the ripe. Poetry comes from the tendency to contemplation. A man with imagination cannot retain the imagination, cannot mould it, cannot build it up unless he has this contemplative tendency within him. The more one contemplates the more one is able to conceive of what one receives. Not only this, but after contemplation a person is able to realize a certain idea more clearly than if that idea had only passed through his mind.

The process of contemplation is like the work of the camera: when the camera is put before a certain object and has been properly focused, then only that object is received by the camera. And therefore when an object before one is limited, then one can see that object more clearly. What constitutes the appeal of the poet is that he tells his readers of something he has seen behind these generally recognized ideas. The prophet goes still further. He not only contemplates one idea, but he can contemplate on any idea: There comes a time in the life of the prophet or of anyone who contemplates, when whatever object he casts his glance upon opens up and reveals to him what it has in its heart. In the history of the world we see that besides their great imagination, their great dreams, their ecstasy and their joy in the divine life, the prophets have often been great reformers, scientists, medical men or even statesmen.

This in itself shows their balance; it shows that theirs is not a one-sided development; they do not merely become dreamers or go into trances, but both sides of their personality are equally development. It is an example of God in man that the prophets manifest. We can see this in the life of Joseph: we are told that he was so innocent, so simple that he went with his brothers, yielding to them, and that this led to his betrayal. In his relationship with Zuleikha we see the human being, the tendency to beauty. And at the same time there is the question he continually asks: What am I doing? What shall I do? Later in his life we see him as one who knows the secret of dreams, as the mystic who interprets the dream of the king. And still later in his life we see that he became a minister, with the administration of the country in his hands, able to carry out the work of the state.

Spirituality has become far removed from material life, and so God is far removed from humanity. Therefore one cannot any more conceive of God speaking through a man, through someone like oneself even a religious man who reads the Bible every day will have great difficulty in understanding the verse, 'Be ye perfect, even as your Father in heaven is perfect.' The Sufi message and its mission are to bring this truth to the consciousness of the world: that man can dive so deep within himself that he can touch the depths where he is united with the whole of life, with all souls, and that he can derive from that source harmony, beauty, peace, and power.

Sufi poetic imagery stands by itself, distinct and peculiar in its character. It is both admired and criticized for its peculiarity. Why it is different from the expressions of other poets born in various countries, is because of its Persian origin and the particular qualities of Persia - the fine climate, the ancient traditions, its being the place where, it is said, wine was tasted for the first time; a land of luxury, a land of beauty, a land of art and imagination. It was natural that with Persian thinkers of all periods, who thought deeply on life, its nature and character, their expressions should become subtle, artistic, fine, and picturesque. In short, it is the dancing of the soul. In all other living beings, the soul is lying asleep, but when once the soul has awakened, called by beauty, it leaps up dancing, and its every movement makes a picture, whether in writing, poetry, music or whatever it may be. A dancing soul will always express the most subtle and intricate harmonies in the realm of music or poetry.

When we read the works of Hafiz and of many other Sufi poets, we shall find that they are full of the same imagery and this is partly because that was the time of Islam. The mission of Islam had a particular object in view, and in order to attain that object it had strict rules about life. A free-thinker had difficulty in expressing his thoughts without being accused of having done a great wrong towards the religion and the State. And these free- thinkers of Persia, with their dancing soul and continual enthusiasm, began to express their soul in this particular imagery, using words such as 'the beloved', 'wine', 'wine-press', and 'tavern'. And this poetry became so popular that not only the wise derived benefit from it, but also the simple ones enjoyed the beauty of its wonderful expressions which make an immediate appeal to every soul. There is no doubt that the souls which were already awakened and those on the point of awakening were inspired by these poems. Souls which were opening their eyes after the deep slumber of many years began to rise up and dance; as Hafiz says, 'If those pious ones of long robes listen to my verse, my song, they will immediately begin to get up and dance'. And then he says at the end of the poem, 'Forgive me, O pious ones, for I am drunk just now!'

This concept of drinking is used in various connections and conveys many different meanings. In the first place, imagine that there is a magic tavern where there are many different kinds of wine. Each wine has a different effect upon the person who drinks it. One drinks a wine which makes him light-hearted, frivolous, humorous; another drinks a wine which makes him sympathetic, kind, tender, gentle. Someone else drinks one which makes him bewildered at everything he sees. Another drinks and finds his way into the ditch. One becomes angry after drinking while another becomes passionate. One drinks and is drowned in despair. Another drinks and begins to feel loving and affectionate; yet another drinks a wine that makes him discouraged with everything. Imagine how interested we should all be to see that tavern! In point of fact we live in that tavern and we see it every day; only, we do not take proper notice of it.

Once I saw a Madzub, (one who is absorbed in a plane of involving consciousness) a man who pretends to be insane, who though living in the world does not wish to be of the world, standing in the street of a large city, laughing. I stood there, feeling curious to know what made him laugh at that moment. And I understood that it was the sight of so many drunken men, each one having had his particular wine.

It is most amusing when we look at it in this way. There is not one single being on earth who does not drink wine; only, the wine of one is different from the wine of the other. A man does not only drink during the day but the whole night long, and he awakens in the morning intoxicated by whatever wine he has been drinking. He awakens with fear or with anger, he awakens with joy, or with love and affection; and the moment he awakens from sleep he shows what wine he has been drinking.

One might ask why the great Sufi teachers have taken such a great interest in the particular imagery of these poets. The reason is that they found the solution to the problem of life by looking upon the world as a tavern, with many wines and each person drinking a different one. They discovered the alchemy, the chemical process, by which to change the wine that a person drinks, and give him another wine to see how this works. The work of the Sufi teacher with his pupil is of that kind. He first finds out which blend of wine his *mureed* (disciple) drinks, and then he finds out which blend be must have.

But, one will ask, is there then no place for soberness in life? There is, but when that soberness is properly interpreted, one sees that it too is wine. Amir (Khusraw), the Hindustani poet, has expressed it in verse, 'The eyes of the sober one spoke to the eyes of the drunken one: "You have no place here, for your intoxication is different from mine."' The awakened person seems to be asleep to the sleeping one, and so the one who has become sober also appears to be still drunk; for the condition of life is such that no one appears to be sober. It is this soberness which is called *Nirvana* by Buddhists and *Mukti* by Hindus.

But if I were asked if it is then desirable for me to be sober, my reply would be, no. What is desirable is for us to know what soberness is, and after knowing what soberness is, then to take any wine we may choose. The tavern is there; wines are there. There are two men: one who is the master of wine, the other who is the slave of wine; the first drinks wine, but wine drinks up the other. The one whom wine drinks up is mortal; he who drinks wine becomes immortal. What is the love of God? What is divine knowledge? Is it not a wine? Its experience is different, its intoxication is different, for there is ordinary wine and there is most costly champagne. The difference is in the wine.

In the imagery of the Sufi poets this tavern (winehouse) is the world, and the Saki (Winebringer) is God. In whatever form the wine-giver comes and gives a wine, it is God who comes. In this way, by recognizing the Saki, the wine-giver, in all forms, the Sufi worships God;. for he recognizes Him in friend and foe as the wine-giver. And wine is that influence which we receive *from* life, an harmonious influence or a depressing influence, a beautiful influence or one that lacks beauty. When we have given in to it then we become drunk, then we become addicted to it, then we are under its influence;

but when we have sought soberness then we have risen above it all, and then all wines are ours.

At all times Persia has had great poets and it has been called the land of poetry; in the first place because the Persian language is so well adapted to poetry, but also because all Persian poetry contains a mystical touch. The literary value of the poetry only makes it poetry; but when a mystical value is added this makes the poetry prophecy. The climate and atmosphere of Persia have also been most helpful to poetry, and the very imaginative nature of the people has made their poetry rich. At all times and in all countries, when the imagination has no scope for expansion, poetry dies and materialism increases.

There is no poet in the world who is not a mystic. A poet is a mystic whether consciously, or unconsciously, for no one can write poetry without inspiration, and when a poet touches the profound depths of the spirit, struck by some aspect of life, he brings forth a poem as a diver brings forth a pearl.

In this age of materialism and ever-growing commercial- ism man seems to have lost the way of inspiration. During my travels I was asked by a well-known writer whether it is really true that there is such a thing as inspiration. This gave me an idea of how far nowadays some writers and poets are removed from inspiration. It is the materialism of the age which is responsible for this; if a person has a tendency towards poetry or music, as soon as he begins to write something his first thought is, 'Will it catch on or not? What will be its practical value?' And generally what catches on is that which appeals to the average man. In this way culture is going downward instead of upward.

When the soul of the poet is intoxicated by the beauty of nature and the harmony of life, it is moved to dance; and the expression of the dance is poetry. The difference between inspired poetry and mechanical writing is as great as the difference between true and false. For long ages the poets of Persia have left a wonderful treasure of thought for humanity. Jelal-ud-Din Rumi has revealed in his *Masnavi* the mystery of profound revelation. In the East his works are considered as sacred as holy scriptures. They have illuminated numberless souls and the study of his work can be considered to belong to the highest standard of culture.

The poet is a creator, and he creates in spite of all that confronts him; he creates a world of his own. And by doing so he rises naturally above that plane where only what is visible and touchable is regarded as real. When he sings to the sun, when he smiles to the moon, when he prays to the sea, and when he looks at the plants, at the forests, and at life in the desert, he communicates with nature. In the eyes of the ordinary person he is imaginative, dreamy, visionary; his thoughts seem to be in the air. But if one asked the poet what he thinks of these others, he would say that it is those who cannot fly who remain on the ground. It is natural that creatures which walk on the earth are not always able to fly; those which fly in the air must have wings, and among human beings one will find that same difference, for in human beings there are all things.

There are souls like germs and worms, there are souls like animals and birds, and there are souls like jinns and angels. Among human beings all can be found: those who belong to the earth, those who dwell in heaven, and those who dwell in the very depths.

Those who were able to soar upward by the power of their imagination have been living poets. What they said was not only a statement, it was music itself; it not only had a rhythm, but it had also a tone in it. It made their souls dance and it would make anyone dance who heard their poetry. Thus Hafiz of Shiraz gives a challenge to the dignified, pious men of his country when he says, 'Pious friends, you would forget your dignity if you would hear the song which came from my glowing heart.' And it is such souls who have touched the highest summits of life, so that they have been able to contribute some truth, giving an interpretation of human nature and the inner law of life.

It is another thing with poets who have made poetry for the sake of fame or name or popularity, or so that it might be appreciated by others; for that is business and not poetry. Poetry is an art, an art of the highest degree. The poet's communication with nature brings him in the end to communicate with himself, and by that communication he delves deeper and deeper, within and without, communicating with life everywhere. This communication brings him into a state of ecstasy, and in his ecstasy his whole being is filled with joy; he forgets the worries and anxieties of life, he rises above the praise and blame of this earth, and the things of this world become of less importance to him. He stands on the earth but gazes into the heavens; his outlook on life becomes broadened and his sight keen. He sees things that no one else is interested in, that no one else sees.

This teaches us that what may be called heaven or paradise is not very far from man. It is always near him, if only he would look at it. Our life is what we look at. If we look at the right thing then it is right; if we look at the wrong thing then it is wrong. Our life made according to our own attitude, and that is why the poet proves to be self-sufficient, and also indifferent and independent; these qualities become wings, for him to fly upward. The poet is in the same position as anyone else in regard to the fears and worries that life brings, the troubles and difficulties that everyone feels in the midst of the world, and yet he rises above these things so that they do not touch him.

No doubt the poet is much more sensitive to the troubles and difficulties of life than an ordinary person. If he took to heart everything that came to him, all the jarring influences that disturbed his peace of mind, all the rough edges of life that everyone has to rub against, he would not be able to go on; but on the other hand if he hardened his heart and made it less sensitive, then he would also close his heart to the inspiration which comes as poetry. Therefore in order to open the doors of his heart, to keep its sensitiveness, the one who communicates with life within and without is open to all influences whether agreeable or disagreeable and is without any protection; and his only escape from all the disturbances of life is through rising above them.

The prophetic message which was given by Zarathushtra (Zoroaster) to the people of Persia was poetic from beginning to end. It is most interesting to see that Zarathushtra showed in his scriptures and all through his life how a poet rises from earth to heaven. It suggests to us how Zarathushtra communicated with nature, with its beauty, and how at every step he took he touched deeper and deeper the depths of life. Zarathushtra formed his religion by praising the beauty in nature and by finding the source of his art which is creation itself in the Artist who is behind it all.

What form of worship did he teach? He taught the same worship with which he began his poetry and with which he finished it. He said to his pupils, 'Stand before the sea, look at the vastness of it, bow before it, before its source and goal.' He said to them, 'Look at the sun, and see what joy it brings. What is at the back of it? Where does it come from? Think of its source and goal, and how you are heading towards it.' People then thought that it was sun-worship, but it was not; it was the worship of light which is the source and goal of all. That communication within and without sometimes extended the range of a poet's vision so much that it was beyond the comprehension of the average man.

When the Shah of Persia said that he would like to have the history of his country written, for one did not exist at that time, Firdausi, a poet who was inspired and intuitive said, 'I will write it and bring it to you.' He began to meditate, throwing his searchlight as far back into the past as possible, and before the appointed time he was able to prepare that book and bring it to the court. It is said that the spiritual power of that poet was so great that when someone at the court sneered at the idea of a man being able to look so far back into the past, he went up to him and put his hand on his forehead and said, 'Now see!' And the man saw with his own eyes that which was written in the book.

This is human; it is not superhuman, although examples of it are rarely to be found; for in the life of every human being, especially of one who is pure-hearted, loving, sympathetic, and good, the past, present, and future are manifested to a certain extent. If one's inner light were thrown back as a searchlight it could go much further than man can comprehend. Some have it to develop this gift, but others are born with it; and among those who are born with it we find some who perhaps know ten or twelve years before and what is going to happen. Therefore a poet is someone who can focus his soul on the past, and also throw his light on the future, and make that clear which has not yet happened but which has been planned beforehand and which already exists in the abstract.

It is such poetry that becomes inspirational poetry. It is through such poetry that the intricate aspects of metaphysics can be taught. All the Upanishads of the Vedas are written in poetry; the suras of the Qu'ran and Zarathushtra's scriptures are all in poetry. All these prophets, whenever they came, ·brought the message in poetry.

The development of poetry in Persia occurred at a time when there was a great conflict between the orthodox and the free-thinkers. At that time the law of the nation was a religious law and no one was at liberty to express his free thoughts which might be in conflict with the religious ideas. And there were great thinkers such as Firdausi, Farid-ud-Din-Attar, Jelal-ud-Din Rumi, Sa'di, Hafiz, Jami, Omar Khayyam, who were not only poets, but who were poetry itself. They were living in another world although they appeared to be on earth. Their outlook on life, their keen sight, were different to those of everyone else. The words which arose from their hearts were not brought forth with effort, they were natural flames rising up out of the heart. And these words remain as flames enlightening souls of all times, whatever soul they have touched.

Sufism has been the wisdom of these poets. There has never been a poet of note in Persia who was not a Sufi, and every one of them has added a certain aspect to the Sufi ideas, but they took great care not to affront the minds of orthodox people.

Therefore a new terminology had to be invented in Persian poetry; the poets had to use words such as 'wine' and 'bowl' and 'beloved' and 'rose', words which would not offend the orthodox mind and would yet at the same time serve as symbolical expressions to explain the divine law." (All in brackets, by Paul Smith).

Further Reading…

The Sufi Message of Hazrat Inayat Khan Volume X: Sufi Mysticism; The Path of Initiation and Discipleship; **Sufi Poetry,** *Art: Yesterday, Today and Tomorrow; The Problem of the Day. Barrie and Jenkins, London, 1964. (Pages 119-154… after the three essays printed above Hazrat Inayat Khan goes on to talk about 'Attar, Rumi, Sadi and Hafiz).*

A History of Ottoman Poetry by E.J.W. Gibb. Volume One, Luzac & Co. Ltd. London 1900. (Pages 33-69.)

A Critical Appreciation of Arabic Mystical Poetry by Dr. S.H. Nadeem, Adam Publishers. New Delhi, 2003.

Sufi Poems, A Medieval Anthology by Martin Lings, Islamic Texts Society, Cambridge, 2004.

The Way of the Mystics: The Early Christian Mystics and The Rise of the Sufis by Margaret Smith, Sheldon Press, 1976.

In the Garden of Myrtles: Studies in Early Islamic Mysticism by Tor Andrae, Translated by Birgitta Sharpe. State University of New York Press, Albany. 1987.

Muslim Saints and Mystics… Episodes from the 'Memorial of the Saints' by Farid al-Din Attar, Translated by A.J. Arberry. Routledge and Kegan Paul, London, 1966.

Kashf Al-Mahjub of Al-Hujwiri. Translated by R.A. Nicholson, Luzac, London. 1967.

The Doctrine of the Sufis by Abu Bakr al-Kalabadhi, Translated by A.J. Arberry, Cambridge University Press 1935.

The Mystics of Islam by Reynold A. Nicholson. Routledge and Kegan Paul, London, reprint 1974.

The Idea of Personality in Sufism by Reynold Alleyne Nicholson, First Published 1923.

The Heritage of Sufism Volume One... Edited by Leonard Lewisohn, Oneworld Publications, Oxford, 1999.

Persian Mysticism by R.P. Masani, Award Publishing House, New Delhi, 1981.

Sufi Literature and the Journey to Immortality by A.E.I. Falconar, Motilal Banarsidass Publishers, Delhi, 1991.

An Introduction to Sufi Doctrine by Titus Burkhardt, Trans. by D.M. Matheson. Sh. Muhammad Ashraf, Lahore, 1973.

Persian Sufi Poetry: An Introduction to the Mystical Use of Classical Poems by J.T.P. De Bruijn. Curzon Press, 1997.

The Drunken Universe: An Anthology of Persian Sufi Poetry, Translation and Commentary by Peter Lamborn Wilson and Nasrollah Pourjavady. Phanes Press, Grand Rapids, 1987.

The Persian Sufis by Cyprian Rice, O.P. George Allen and Unwin Ltd, London, 1964.

God Speaks: The Theme of Creation and Its Purpose by Meher Baba. Dodd, Mead & Company, New York, 1955. (Meher Baba in great detail explains the Involution of the Soul and the seven stages of the Spiritual Path, the role of the Perfect Master, the Creation and the different States of God using quotations from Sufi poets and Masters and Sufi terminology and cross-referencing with Christian Mystical and Vedantic terminology. Meher Baba also quotes various couplets by Hafiz when describing the passage through the inner planes of consciousness to God-Realization).

The Hebraic Tongue Restored By Fabre d'Olivet. English Trans. by Nayan Louise Redfield. G.P. Putnam's & Sons. N.Y. 1921 (Fabre D'Olivet reconstructed ancient Hebrew and then faithfully translated Genesis... by using the Adamic Alphabet and revealed that its sounds really told the Divine love-story between Adam and Eve... in a spiral, also the form of the ghazal. See also my book and filmscript on Fabre D'Olivet and his miraculous powers of healing deaf mutes by blowing into their ears the original creative sound of original Adamic vowels... The Healer and the Emperor).

Hallaj teaching.

Qit'as...

Yes, go and tell, for the deep Sea I sailed,

that my ship has gone down, far offshore.

By Holy Cross I must go to death of me,

to the Holy Cities I can go to... no more.

I searched the world for a place to call home,

but upon the earth no such a place did I see.

My desires I obeyed and they trapped me...

if with my fate I was contented, I'd be free!

Hear my sorrow, O You, for souls whose witness now:

leave, to go beyond, until into the Witness of Eternity!

Hear my sorrow, O You... for the miracles whose logic

shut argument's mouth, in name of Your love's ardency!

O hear my sorrow... O You... for all of those who rode

themselves as steeds... all the bravery of silent chivalry:

for all them who have been lost, like that vanished tribe

of Ad and their lost Garden of Iram: gone, completely!*

And, after them, the abandoned herd... wandering and

stumbling, blinder than beasts, or she-camels may be!

*Note: The garden of Iram was said to have been created by King Shudad, the son of Ad who was the grandson of Iram, who was the son of Shem, Noah's son. The tribe of Ad settled in the desert near Aden and Ad started to build a fabulous city that was finished by his son Shudad. Shudad created a wonderful garden around his palace that he thought would rival the Garden of Paradise. When it was finished he set out to admire it and when he came near to it all were destroyed by a great sound that came from God. It is said that the ruins still exist near Aden. This poem is said to have been recited by Hallaj on the night before his execution.

If you met me tonight in clothes of real poverty,

be assured that by being on my back threadbare,

this clothing has bestowed on me, real Freedom;

so do not be misled, if you see me like this, here,

different from the past: I have a soul and it must

either perish or rise to a destiny beyond compare.

Wanting the truth, I thought hard about the religions...

I discovered that one root with many branches are they.

It makes good sense not to make one follow a religion...

in case it stops any one from root that in depth does lay.

So, allow that root to claim that one, that root where all

meanings and perfection are opened... to be clear, as day.

O my only One, make me one with You, for no way
can reach Your Oneness, even faith can't hold sway.
The Truth I am... Truth, and the Truth is the Truth,
clothed in Its Essence, separation can't have its way.
See manifested the dawn's light from Your Presence
shining brilliantly, a lightning flash, from every ray!

You live inside my heart; in there are secrets about You:

Your house is good; no, good is the One found by You!

The only secret in there is You, there's no other I know:

with Your Vision look, other than You is one there too?

Whether the night of separation should be short or long,

my closest friend is my hope of You, remembering You.

I'm so happy if it makes You happy to be destroying me

because whatever You choose, my Killer... I choose too!

Heart of You is where a Name of Yours is hidden,
and it is not perceived by light nor by the darkness,
and on seeing light of Your face I see the Mystery:
all Goodness and all Excellence, all Mercifulness.
Beloved, take now this word of mine: You know it,
but the Tablet doesn't; and Pen, not yet, I confess!

This soul of mine had different desires...
but since seeing You they jelled into one.
Those I envied now envy me, as I'm lord
of others, since You my Lord did become.
Due to You they scolded me, my friends,
foes, ignorantly... trying of me, was done.
I have left to men their religion and world
for Your Love, my world and my religion!

I feel no separation... distance from You I do not feel:

it's now my belief that near or far are the same thing.

For me, if I'm separated from You, it's my companion:

not only that, but... as we are one, can it be existing?

Praise to You for where You are from in Your essence;

to Your pure servant, who only to You is prostrating.

You've gone from me but not yet from my conscience,
inside it You're all of my joy and all of my happiness.
When You went, leaving was Your going to leave me
because for me absence became the same as presence,
because You stay in the secret thoughts inside of me,
there... beyond imagination, hidden in my conscience.
It's true that You are my closest friend in the daytime
and I intimately talk with You, through the darkness.

Your will be done, my Lord and my Master!

Your will be done, my purpose and meaning!

O essence of my being, O goal of my desire:

O my speech, O my hints and my gesturing!

O All of my all, O my hearing and my sight,

O my whole, my element, my atoms uniting!

Your place inside my heart is all of my heart:

there is no room for any others in Your place.

Between skin and bone my soul You placed,

what could I do, if I lost You... You replace?

I wrote, but did not write to You... writing
to my Soul what cannot be written I wrote.
Between You as Soul and one who loves it
there's no difference, it's You by me. Note,
that naught I wrote... it all comes from You
to You, replying to You: no answer I quote.

Your Love, I hold with all of my being... You are my sanctuary: to me You're showing You, like You are inside me, and if I am turning my heart to another, that I see some alien is true: so, I realize my ease with You: me as in life's prison, men surrounding, so take me... to You!

The Lights in humans are from Lights of religion's Light,

and the Secret is the Secrets in the souls secret insight…

and in all beings is the Being, the Being that says, "BE!"

This heart of mine is chosen, reserved… with it, so tight!

Think deeply upon what I say with the eye of the mind…

the mind is so wanting to be hearing and to have insight!

I've found You within me, yet my tongue calls You:

united in one way, we are also separated in another.

For, while Your majesty conceals You from my eyes,

deep inside my heart ecstasy has brought You closer.

O You, subtle Secret of my secret… You are veiled
from all beings imagination on which life's prevailed:
still, inside and out You have completely manifested
Yourself in each thing to each thing that has existed.
It would be ignorance for me to ask anything of You,
it'd be to doubt, obviously, lack of You being trusted!
O You Absolute Existence, You are not other than I:
how can I possibly for myself, from me… have asked?

With the eye of my heart I saw my Creator:

I said, "Who are You?" You replied, "You!"

So... like from You, there is nowhere... and

there is no where too, when it is about You!

No image You reveal, for one to imagine...

imagination needs to imagine where is You!

That One is You, Who filled Everywhere...

and beyond where, too... so, where are You?

My annihilation's end is in my annihilation,

and in my annihilation is discovered... You!

Whoever seeks God, taking his intellect for a guide,
remaining perplexed God sends him away... so far:
with wild confusion He confounds his inmost heart,
so that distraught he cries, "I know not, *if* You are!"

Your Soul, is mixed with my soul…
like musk is mixed with ambergris,
when perfumes blend: so, what You
touch touches me… we are, together!

O you who go on blaming me for loving that One,

how hard you can be, still are: O if only you knew

how that One helps, you would me never blame...

others have their pilgrimage... and I have one too,

to that Guest in me: they may be offering animals

as a sacrifice... that I offer blood of heart, is true!

There are a people who not by the feet go around:

they circle God, are all excused from *Kaaba*, too!

Is there anything on earth that is without You
that they would go up to Heaven to You see?
Dazzled by Your light You see them looking,
their sight is so lost that You they do not see!

If the shadow has got you in its grip...
then out into light of heart's peace go.
If who you are you don't know... lost,
listen to Beloved, "I am you, know!"
Your name you'll forget, and home...
know you are no one, found: it is so!
Found, but not by one who will brag
of such many rescues... O no, O no!
Found by One who reveals nothing
and secretly guides. to Love's flow!
At heart one may throw a blood-red
rose; symbol of separation long ago!

O my God, with this illness what am I to do?

When doctors see me coming, they're leaving!

They shout out, "Let your sickness, cure you!"

With sickness, can one who is sick, be curing?

O God, because of Love I've become so tired:

about this, how can I, to You be complaining?

This pain that I have is from soul's suffering:

it's I, myself... this sickness goes on causing!

Glory to that One Who humanity created
as the secret of His Divine Light, shining.
And then that One was appearing for His
creation in form of one eating and drinking.
Until that One's creatures glanced at Him
that from one eyebrow to another, is going!

Love, in pre-eternity, from the very start…

from inside it and due to it, it is appearing.

Love, before time began, is an attribute of

that One, Whose victims now are living!

They, are from in that One, beyond time:

while the transitory on time is depending.

That One summoned Love upon creation

as an attribute, so… a spark was shining.

With *Alif* as partner, *Lam* was formed…

both, as One, were before the beginning!

In separating them they are two to unite,

as with slave and Lord they are differing.

Truly, desire's fire with Truth enflames…

no matter how near or far, they are being.

The more infatuated, the more they fade;

the strong are humbled, if hearts losing.

---

*Note: This poem refers to the Covenant that God made on the First Day
i.e. before the Creation, in God's Imagination. God created (in His Infinite
Imagination) all the souls that were possible to create, and He asked them:
"Am I NOT your God?" This of course was something of a trick question,
and not without a sense of humour. Some, out of love, not wishing to be
rude by not answering answered: "Yes!" (In other words: You are NOT our
God). These were the lovers of God. Others did not answer. God then
manifested all of the souls into creation, some of them being lovers, and
others, those who had to learn from the lovers to try to love and to say
"yes" to God, even though to try is the best that one can do.*

Love that's hidden is continually at risk...
from confronting fears, comes true peace.
If one talks about love that is kept secret,
it's like the fire in stone hiding... useless!
And when the police and the jailor arrive,
tellers of tales about me go on telling lies.
I feel like I want to be freed of Your love,
but I'd need to not hear or to see, no less!

Friend, you played; time's gone to play with old heads:
you won game, broke heart's secret, but time's healing.
These eyes wherein desires used to grow, are dimmed;
heart, where love's memories fought, are not fighting.
You're there now, pulled down with the enemies, lost:
you do not visit here anymore, so you I am not seeing.
The same way the donkey went carrying Umm 'Amr:
she never came back again, donkey wasn't returning.

In eye of my heart I did see my Lord…
I said, "Without a doubt it's truly You.
In everything it is only You that I see,
through all I see nothing but You, too.
Every place that exists You only own;
and yet… that no place is You, is true!
Still, if You were to designate a place,
there, would give information on You!
If You, there was a way of imagining;
imagination, it would know You, too.
I understand all, so all that I'm seeing
as 'I' am annihilated. can be only You!
O Lord, please bless and forgive me…
for that I'm seeking only You is true!"

My heart's disturbed due to four letters,

also my longing and mind and grieving:

Alif... by which actions are stimulated,

Lam: that one towards guilt is leading.

Lam... my meaning is increased by it...

Ha... makes me understand, be loving. *

*Note: These four letters are spelling out 'Allah'.

Calm followed by silence, then words by accident:
then comes knowledge, drunkenness, obliteration!
Earth is followed by fire, and then light appears...
from cold shade's appearing, then sun shines upon.
A road of thorns, a path appears and wilderness...
now a river appears, then ocean, a shore to step on.
And then there is contentment, longing, then love,
and then there's nearness, loving, then unification.
Then closing followed by opening... then nothing:
then being apart, together, then... desire comes on!
These are the signs for those who can understand,
who the world as almost worthless they look upon.

O You sun, O You moon, You daytime...
my heaven and my hell is You, only You!
It would be sinful to give up for You, sin!
Anyone leaving You would be empty, too!
They for You give away all begging ways,
but what of the one who can't help it, too?

I'm astonished at me and You;

O You, goal of all my longing!

You let me, to You come close,

though You 'me' I was calling.

Finding You, I was losing me:

in You, me You were effacing!

You are the blessing of my life

and after death my consoling!

Only You, are caring for me...

my fear You go on comforting.

You, are the garden of Truth...

now, my talents are blooming!

If there's anything that I want

that desire's You to be having!

There's a pearl in the depth of my heart,

it's a pearl that can't be touched by me.

And, when doubts steal into my mind,

I begin to tremble... something terribly.

My Beloved, has given to me this as a

present to keep in confidence, secretly.

And by it I'm able to see, though blind:

I'm given wisdom though I act naively.

This love by 'seven sleepers' is known:

those seven are friends, I hold dearly.*

In the shadow of their mountain time

is stopping like it has stopped for me!

My Beloved, returns in its silence...

comes back to claim pearl, rightfully!

*Note: Seven Sleepers, refers to Christian youths who hid inside a cave in a mountain outside the city of Ephesus around 250 AD, to escape a persecution of the Roman emperor Decius. Having fallen asleep in the cave, they awoke approximately 150-200 years later. The story has its highest prominence in the Muslim world; it is told in the Koran [18, 9-26] While not giving the number of youths involved, the story largely parallels the Christian account. This version includes a dog that accompanied the youths into the cave, and kept watch at the entrance for the entire time.

Lamp of the Divine Light is the science of Prophecy...
ecstatic inspiration's spark is in grave God digs for it!
By God, breathing into my skin's breath of His Spirit,
breathing a note that Israfil will blow, to end this pit!*
When One is transformed before my soul so as to talk
to me, upon Mt Sinai I see Moses... in my ecstatic fit!

*Note: Israfil, the Angel of the Trumpet, holds his holy trumpet to his lips
century after century, awaiting the signal from God to sound it at the Last
Judgment.

Between me and the Truth, there is no longer
explanation, or proof, or signs to convince me.
A vision of God is shining here... like a flame
that's magnificent in its shining sovereignty!
One only knows God to who God is known:
an illusion that passes, can't know Divinity.
In other words, the Creator cannot be taken
from what the Creator creates… obviously!
Can't you see, a passing being turned away
from that One is away… for all of Eternity?
The One is proof, from the One, to the One
and in the One is the Witness, essentially...
of the Reality in the Revelation that can tell,
can perceive what's good, what's evil totally.
God is the proof, from God, in God, for God:
in Truth we found It, in Its outer form we see.
This is my existence, my evidence, my belief:
this is the Oneness, explaining God's Unity!
In this way we express our being One in God,
we who all know the One openly and secretly.
This is the height of all intoxicated by God…
the people of God, soul's companions... of me!

Now, becoming evident to you...
is a well-kept secret's revelation.
On your darkness a dawn breaks:
your heart's veil, the secret upon!
God wouldn't be revealed to you
if you kept to yourself, on and on.
But when you destroy your heart
God enters, gives His revelation.
With this, a dialogue will follow,
its words to Us taste to chew on.

In creation, there are hearths and fires of faith,

and in hearts that can keep secrets, conscience.

For Being in depth of us beings is the creating

Existence, holding heart that wants Essence!

What I am saying with mind's eye consider…

as the mind can listen, see, know consequence!

O friend I've been immersed in a deep sea,

I'm not Husayn, as him don't think of me!

See me as near God, I am God, I am God!

From all greed, hatred and pride I am free!

'I don't blame me as blame from me is far:

please help me Lord because alone is me!

True, is the promise; Your promise is true

and hard at the beginning of my destiny!'

Here is my letter needing to be inscribed:

read it and then know that I a martyr be!

I try to hard to be waiting patiently...
but this heart, can it ever be patient?
To mine Your spirit has joined itself
in closeness, and in being… distant.
And so it's true that I'm You as You
are me and that which I always want.

I wish for You, but not to get a reward...
to get punishment for You I am wishing.
From all of this I obtained what I desire,
except for joy of my passion in suffering.

One night the sun rose up of the One I love,

it shone on and about setting nothing knew:

because the sun of the day enhances night...

and the sunbird of the heart away new flew.

Passions of the Truth that are entirely born of Truth,
but... that cannot attain the highest understanding:
what is passion but an inclination followed by a look,
that among those minds the flame goes on spreading?
And if Truth should come and then inhabit the mind
three states increase compared to those of foreseeing:
a state that annihilates mind in essence of its desire,
then renders one into a state that's deeply confusing;
a state where all forces of the mind becomes knotted
on turning to a sight annihilating all who are seeing.

Ah, you breeze, to the gazelle be saying...
"My thirst will be worse from drinking!"
I've a Beloved, His love, guts surround...
and if He wants, on them He's treading.
His spirit is my spirit, my soul His soul:
He wishes I wish, I wish He is wishing!

I never stop floating in the sea of love,
up and down the waves are lifting me.
Sometimes those waves lift me up and
sometimes I'm choosing to be gloomy.
Then finally He is leading me to love,
there... where there is no shore to see.
I call Him Whose Name I do not tell,
and Who in love isn't betrayed by me.
What my love doesn't wish for, Lord,
is not in our pact... and will never be.

When I remember You, nostalgia almost kills me
and my absence from You is grief… and sadness.
Each part of me is now a heart that implores You,
that quickly succumbs to pain, grief and distress.

Ghazals…

By God I'm swearing the sun never sets or is rising
when out of love for You, each breath I'm breathing.
And, when ever I go off with friends to have a talk,
as we sit about You is the one thing I'm discussing.
And all my thoughts are only on You, happy or sad:
only You are in my heart; "You," I'm remembering.
And when I'm thirsting I don't think to drink water
unless… in that cup that face of Yours I am seeing!
And, if I could possibly come to You, then I would
rush, either on my face, or even on my head walking.

Is it I, or is it You? The two, gods numbering two!

It is not up to me to be claiming that there are two!

For eternity is Your Self, in the nothingness of me:

the Everything that is mine, knows illusion as two!

Your Essence is where? From where am I to identify

when nowhere is mine… that, is really obvious, too?

And Your face, which with my eyesight I may seek,

either in the vision of my heart… or eyes sight too?

Between You and me is an 'I AM' overcoming me…

using Your 'I AM' take mine, from between us, too.

I've a Beloved I visit when I am alone completely,

He is always available though Him one can't see.

You will never see me lending an ear to that One

to be listening to any words He might say openly,

because His words have no form, are not spoken…

and, they are not like any voices making a melody.

It is like I am my own go-between, communicating

through my inspiration with my essence, inwardly!

That One is here, away, near and distant: to try to

describe or encompass Him, is… an impossibility!

Imagine, that One is nearer than one's conscience,

and even than inspiration's flashes… closer, in me!

See… I'm here, O You, my secret, my surety:
see, I'm here, O You my goal, the end of me!
I call to You… no, You're calling me to You:
can I talk to You, if You'd not talked to me?
You are my soul's Essence, what I aim for…
You cause me to speak, O my voice, all I see!
You're the All of my all, my ear and eyesight:
You are my everything, my parts, my totality!
O Everything of my everything, my enigma…
I try to tell All, the profound I say unclearly!
From You, soul was before, dying of ecstasy:
that promise You made me will be end of me!
O Guest, O You One Whom I wait upon…
O soul's food, Life in both worlds, obviously.
My eyes, my ears, may heart be my ransom!
Why do I have to wait to be alone… tell me?
Although You are before my eyes its hidden:
my heart sees You from my lack of proximity.

O You, You are the One that I am seeking,
and in my heart that One that I'm desiring.
Absolute Being, You're the Complete One,
Who I with each bit or part of me, is loving!
From grief and longing I am turning to You:
for You my heart's in claws of a bird, flying.
Lost in shock, rocked by the agony I'm in…
from one wilderness to another, I am going.
By Your mystery I'm blinded as I travel on,
it is always moving… as fast as lightning!
It could be likened to a vision's quickness…
that after one is wakes up, is disappearing.
By that river of consciousness, taken off…
for, that Absolute Being needs satisfying.

With the eye of knowledge I direct my sight,

I've not a single doubt that my sight is right.

Far away from any meaning or doubting too,

this one's conscience is purified by the light!

On the waves of thinking I'm moving along,

I am like an arrow that has a target in sight.

With the wings of longing my heart's flying,

by the wind of my aim I'm traveling… light!

To the One I go Whom I'm afraid to talk of;

not saying Who, in riddles I hide my plight.

I roam the desert until beyond all limits I go,

but… not over the edge, I know what's right!

Then to that One's Will I bow like a slave…

with Love heart is branded: *ah,* such might!

In such closeness my true self I then lose…

so who I am, I am made to forget, outright!

When, over you is riding the steed of loneliness...
and swallowing all hope is despair's cry, no less;
into your left hand take the armour of humility...
into your right hand be taking the spear of tears!
It's important, to be of your lower self cautious...
watchful of its unseen retribution causing stress.
When, in the darkness you must be going along,
under the lamp of purity, be sheltering... no less!
Say to Beloved, "See, my shattered condition...
before we are destined to meet forgive my mess!
O my Beloved, from me don't be far, separated;
before the end don't give up on me, me... bless!"

Ruba'is...

In denying You, it is You I sanctify;

my reason in You, is madness, say I.

Who's Adam, if that one isn't You?

Who in the banished Satan does lie?

I'm the One I love, the One I love is

me,

we are two spirits that live... in one

body.

If you see me, then... you see that One...

and, if you see that One... both, you

see.

A secret, hidden for a long time, is told to

you…

from the dark of night, from you, a day dawns

too:

the veil of the heart over its secret mystery is

you,

it would never have been sealed if not for you,

too.

My host was generous as I was entertained

at the high table… but as cups were passed,

he called for winding-sheet and the scimitar:

to drink with dragon in summer is so fated. *

*Note: This was the final poem Hallaj uttered.

Qasidas...

My faithful friends… kill me,
to kill me is to alive make me.
To destroy all trace of my life
is my highest goal… you see.
To stay in my lower self, is a
a sin I cannot of repenting be.
My life, due to my lower self,
is destroyed: I'm lost, totally!
So, my friends, take my life…
burn my poor bones, entirely!
Then, when by my corpse they
walk in graveyards unhappily,
they will find Friend's secret,
in the inner folds… it will be!
I am a shaikh at one moment
and one of the highest degree,
then I'm a small child who on
a nurse is depending entirely.
Or, I am in a box fast asleep,
under the black earth lies me.
My mother birthed her father
it was a wonder that I did see.

And my daughters that I made
like this were the sisters of me,
not in this world full of time...
nor, by any thing like adultery!
So, get together all the parts...
bits of forms that shine to see,
or, that of air, and of fire too...
some water without impurity,
and sow all in soil that's dry...
then watering it from cups be,
of maids that lovingly serve...
streams, flowing refreshingly.
And when seven days pass by
a perfect plant will grow to see!

I am here O my secret, true One, You can see me!
You called me and I came, O my hope and reality!
I go on calling to You... no, it is You to me calling:
Am I saying it is You, or, You saying, "It's Me"?
You're as far as I have to go, Spring of all springs:
You're my reason for being, all my words set free!
All that I am you are, all I see and I hear is You...
You are the universe and the smallest thing to me.
You are totality of what I am and a mystery it is:
the small thing I am confuses You, so hard to see!
You I've always loved and at times I've been hurt
when You've let You to be love's prisoner, in me.
Though I choose to be, I mourn for being an exile:
because of the grief I have my enemies are happy.
I am excited by being afraid as I get close to You:
in depth of my heart it is my longing calming me.
With this One I love so much, what am I to do?
All the doctors tell me from my illness they flee!
I'm weakened, consumed by this love for God...
how to say to that One, "You, did this to me"?
My heart sees when I look but how to be telling
the ways of that One, but by actions... silently?

It's this 'I' of mine that's wrong, a woeful thing!
I am the creator of this condition… this, agony!
I am like someone who is drowning in the ocean
who is reaching out for help with fingertips only.
That one alone who has reached depth of heart,
only that one reaches depth of such melancholy.
You know what I know in this unending illness:
in Yours… I'll find death and resurrection of me.
O You, my hope, my prayers, my abode, breath:
You… my religion and in the end my Destiny…
tell me, "I've saved you!" O my eyes and ears…
why, do You still keep me away, in this agony?
Even though, to my sight You remain hidden…
still my heart can off in the distance, You… see!

APPENDIX

A Selection of Poetry from the Persian, Turkish & Pushtu poets about or influenced by Mansur Hallaj.

(Note: All of the poems below are couplets from longer poems in the forms of the *ghazal, qi'ta, masnavi, qasida)*

ABU SA'ID (968-1049) was a Perfect Master and a poet who lived in Nishapur and composed only *ruba'is,* over 400 of them. He was one of the founders of Persian Sufi and Dervish poetry and a major influence on the *ruba'i* and most poets that followed, especially Sana'i, Nizami, 'Attar and Rumi.

Translation from…

Ruba'iyat of Abu Sa'id. Translation & Introduction by Paul Smith, New Humanity Books, Campbells Creek 2010.

> Mansur Hallaj, a crocodile in Unification's
>
> river…
>
> effaced himself and with the Absolute was a
>
> uniter.
>
> "I'm the Absolute Truth," one day he was declaring:
>
> so where was the Almighty One and where
>
> Mansur?

ANSARI (1005-1090). The great mystical poet Khwaja Abdullah Ansari who passed from this world 1089 in Herat is most famous for his biographical dictionary on saints and Sufi masters and his much loved collection of inspiring prayers, the *Munajat*. His *ruba'is* appear throughout his works.

Translation from...

Ansari: Selected Poems, Translation & Introduction by Paul Smith,
New Humanity Books, Campbells Creek, 2008.
Ruba'iyat of Ansari, Translation & Introduction by Paul Smith,
New Humanity Books, Campbells Creek, 2009.

> "I am God," Hallaj said and the gibbet
>
> crowned:
>
> "God," Abdullah exclaimed, was met...
>
> crowned.
>
> I have also said what was said by Hallaj:
>
> Hallaj said it out loud, I inside, yet...
>
> crowned!

*

MU'IN (1141-1230) Muhammad Mu'inuddin Chishti was also known as *Gharib Nawaz* or 'Benefactor of the Poor', he is the most famous Sufi saint and poet of the Chishti Order of the

Indian Subcontinent. He introduced and established the order in South Asia. The initial spiritual chain of the Chishti order in India, comprising himself, Bakhtiyar Kaki, Baba Farid and Nizamuddin Auliya (each successive person being the disciple of the previous one), constitutes the great Sufi saints of Indian history.

Translation from…

Mu'in ud-din Chishti: Selected Poems, Translation & Introduction by Paul Smith, New Humanity Books, Campbells Creek, 2012.

It wasn't only Mansur who was drunk on love's wine,
the scaffold to the rope the same tale was telling…
"It is all that One!"
The heart freely tells the secret of love and isn't afraid,
as it knows that in what is seen and what's hiding.
it is all that One!

Lift veil of dust and water from off the face of heart and soul,
so that all the darkness of your existence into the light is
turning.
Whoever drinks cup of Eternity in this assembly of existence
holds the rope of Union with God… and the scaffold is
ascending.

If with the eyes of the lover You could see Your beauty...
like me You'd be thinking of only You... night and
day!
Mu'in desires the wine that will take him from himself,
so like Mansur he will unite with You... straight
away.

A drop from Love's ocean was source of Mansur's state:
anything else into the lover's cup to be tasted,
is what?
O Mu'in, if with tongue you speak of God's mysteries...
such a one's place is not a pulpit... the gibbet
is what!

From the cup of Union with God give me a drink,
so in this passing world another Mansur
I am.
Give me from cup which secret of 'I am God' may
come from my tongue and excused forever
I am.

*

'ATTAR (d. 1230). Farid al-din 'Attar is the Perfect Master Poet who was the author of over forty books of poetry and prose including *The Conference of the Birds, The Book of God,* and *The Lives of the Saints.* Apart from his many books in *masnavi* form he also composed many hundreds of mystical *ghazals* and *ruba'is.* He also changed the evolution of the *ruba'i* form by composing a long Sufi epic, the *Mukhtar-nama,* where each *ruba'i* is connected to the one before, something which Fitzgerald attempted to do with those he attributed to Omar Khayyam over six hundred years later.

He was killed by the Mongol invaders outside the gates of Nishapur when at over a hundred years old he advanced on them alone, sword in hand. It is said that after his head was cut off he kept on fighting. In his masterpiece long *masnavi* poem *Ilahi-nama,* 'Book of God, that was to influence Jalal-al-Din Rumi in the composing of his six book masterpiece *Masnavi.*

Translation from...

Ruba'iyat of 'Attar. Translation & Introduction by Paul Smith, New Humanity Books, Campbells Creek, 2009.
'Attar: Selected Poetry. Translation, Introduction & Notes by Paul Smith, New Humanity Books, Campbells Creek, 2010.

If you want to know Love's mystery give up faith

and infidelity: Love comes and makes both, expire.

Thousands of travellers on Love's road lay claim:

in this circle of the way, Hallaj is the gem on fire.

It is a difficult and great task, this mystical path…

thousand travellers, but just one sees Path, entire.

*

RUMI (1207-1273). Jalal-ud-din Rumi was born in Balkh. He moved when about eleven with his family away from Balkh so as to avoid the warlike Mongols. They travelled to Baghdad, to Mecca on pilgrimage, to Damascus and eventually settled near Konya in what is now western Turkey.

On the road to Anatolia, Jalal-ud-din and his father had encountered one of the most famous mystic Persian poets, Farid al-din 'Attar, in the city of Nishapur. 'Attar immediately recognized the boy's spiritual status.

For nine years, Rumi practiced Sufism as a disciple of his father Burhan-ud-din until his father died in 1240. During this period Rumi travelled to Damascus and is said to have spent four years there. While there he first caught a glimpse of the *Qutub* (Perfect Master) Shams-e Tabriz. Rumi's love and his great longing for Shams found expression in music, dance, songs and poems in his collection of poems/songs or *Divan* which he named after his Master... *Divan of Shams-e Tabriz.* This vast work included thousands of *ghazals* and other poetic forms and nearly two thousand *ruba'is* that he would compose for many years, before he became a God-realized Perfect Master. Rumi's disciple Hesam'odin Hasan urged Rumi to write the *'Masnavi'* in the style of Sana'i and 'Attar. Rumi completed six books (35,000 couplets) of these before he died.

Translation from...

Rumi: Selected Poems, Translation & Introduction by Paul Smith, New Humanity Books, Campbells Creek, 2009.

> Every true lover is likened to Mansur, in that they killed
> themselves:
> reveal any one but a lover, who deliberately, himself is
> exterminating!
> A hundred requisitions are made by Death every day upon
> mankind...
> the lover of God, without asking for anything, himself is
> slaying.

One who gets mixed up in Your Love for even a
moment
will experience personal disaster to an incredible
extent.
When Mansur Hallaj revealed Love's Secret...
he was hung by the throat of rope of that zealous
establishment.

It is a party... do not be here without
tambourine...
get up, the drum beat, we're Mansur
obviously.
We're intoxicated, but not from wine:
we're far from anything you thought to
be!

Wool-carder Hallaj, who... " I am the Truth," declared;
swept God's dust from each road, on which he stepped.
And... when that one in the sea of non-existence dived,
he won for us Pearl when he... "I am the Truth," said.

YUNUS EMRE (d. 1321). Yunus Emre is considered by many to be one of the most important Turkish poets excising a great influence on Turkish literature from his own time until the present. He is one of the first known poets to have composed in Turkish of his own age and region rather than in Persian or Arabic, his diction remains very close to the popular speech of his contemporaries in Central and Western Anatolia. Little can be said for certain of his life other than that he was a Sufi dervish of Anatolia. His poetry expresses a deep personal mysticism and humanism and love for God.

He was a contemporary of Rumi, who lived in the same region. Rumi composed his collection of stories and songs for a well-educated urban circle of Sufis, writing primarily in the literary language of Persian. Yunus Emre, on the other hand, traveled and taught among the rural poor, singing his songs in the Turkish language of the common people. A story is told of a meeting between the two great souls: Rumi asked Yunus Emre what he thought of his great work the *Masnavi*. Yunus Emre said, "Excellent, excellent! But I would have done it differently." Surprised, Rumi asked how. Yunus replied, "I would have written, 'I came from the eternal, clothed myself in flesh, and took the name Yunus.'" That story perfectly illustrates Yunus Emre's simple, direct approach that has made him so beloved. Interestingly, the name Yunus means 'dolphin' in Turkish.

Translations from…

Yunus Emre: Selected Poems, Translation & Introduction by Paul Smith, New Humanity Books, Campbells Creek, 2010.

Before time began I was Mansur, that's the reason I'm here:
toss my ashes into the sky, 'Ana'l-Hakk' they'll be spelling,
brother.
Not burnt though fire burns, not chocked but noose hangs…
I go where my work's done: I'm here on just a quick outing,
brother.

For Abraham I made the fire of Nimrod into a vineyard:
disbelief appeared… one who again fire was lighting
is Me!
It was I who said with Hallaj, "I am the living Truth!"
That one who the rope around his neck was placing,
is Me.
When Mustafa, God's beloved, started on the Ascent…
my soul I humbled then and His mystery perceiving,
is Me.

My name is now Yunus at another time it was Isma'il...
for the Beloved, to be a sacrifice, Ararat ascending,
is Me.

Take me to the gallows like Mansur, show me You clearly:
let me sacrifice soul, let me not deny love, let me Love
know.
For agony the remedy is Love, my life I gave up for Love...
Yunus Emre says, "Not for a moment, let me Love
forego!"

Here, those who continually burn are transformed into Light:
that fire is not like any other... there are no flames, not one
sign.
All drunk at that One's gathering sing... "I am the Truth"
like a hundred Hallaj Mansurs: lowest as mad, one could
define.

*

IBN YAMIN (1286-1368) Amir Fakhr al-Din Mahmud, or Ibn
Yamin, was born in Turkistan. His father was a successful
poet who taught him the craft and when he died in 1322 left his

son wealthy and the role of the court-poet in Khurasan. Ibn Yamin was taken captive when war broke out in 1342 and his royal patron was defeated and his complete *Divan* of poems was destroyed or lost (see the first of the *qit'as* below). Thankfully we still have some of his somewhat cynical *ruba'is*. During the last 25 years of his life he composed a further 5000 couplets.

Translation from...

The Wisdom of Ibn Yamin: Selected Poems, Translation & Introduction by Paul Smith, New Humanity Books, 2011.

If a palace with nine gilded porches is your desire,

from five senses, four elements, let it be said:

"Depart!"

You'll find no resting place in the abode of pride:

from the gibbet like some Mansur, tortured,

depart.

A snake's no friend for some rich stone inside it:

uproot your greed and from the snake's head

depart!

HAFIZ (1320-1392). Persia's greatest exponent of the *ghazal* and many believe the greatest poet of all time. Shams-ud-din Mohammed (Hafiz), ugly and small, became a God-Realized Perfect Master *(Qutub)*, was twice exiled from his beloved Shiraz for his criticism of rulers and false Sufi masters (such as Shaikh Ali Kolah) and the hypocritical clergy. He was by far the greatest influence on the poets of his time including Obeyd Zakani (possibly his former teacher). His most gifted student, Jahan Khatun (to follow), composed many *ghazals* based on his and praised him in a number of them.

He has been one of the greatest influences in every way on poets, mystics, philosophers and artists in both the East and West. (See my chapter on 'Hafiz's Influence on the East and the West' in my *Divan of Hafiz*).

His *Divan* shows he composed in other forms other than the *ghazal* that he perfected... including his famous *masnavis* 'Book of the Winebringer' and 'Book of the Minstrel' and 'The Wild Deer'... as well as *ruba'is* of which about 150 have come down to us. As with his immortal *ghazals*, his *ruba'is* are sometimes mystical and sometimes critical of the hypocrisy of his times. Apart from *ruba'is* and *ghazals* he composed his masterpiece *masnavis*, *qit'as*, *qasidas* and a quite wonderful and unique *mukhammas*.

Translations from…

Divan of Hafiz: English Version & Introduction by Paul Smith
New Humanity Books 1986. New Humanity Books 2006

At the Beginning, love and drunkenness seemed O so easy…
but in the end the soul tired and worn out from the chase is.
This subtlety, sweet singing Hallaj sang before decapitation:
"To question theologians now, the wrong time and place is."
I have given my heart to a Friend, fair and bold and delicate,
Who having an agreeable disposition, such pure grace has.

Those on gallows like Mansur obtain desired remedy:
those delving into thinking of a remedy, find pain too
distressing.
When those longing beg in that Presence, grace comes to
this Court They call Hafiz, when, They cause him to be
dying.

My blood will write 'I am The Truth' *[Anal Haq]* on the earth,
if like Mansur they kill me on the gallows, mercilessly, tonight.
Beloved, You possess Divine Wealth, I'm beggar at Your door,
give the gift of Your Glory, make me blissfully happy tonight.

All the time I'm frightened that Hafiz will be lost, obliterated;

for every moment I am in possession of such ecstasy, tonight.

*

JAHAN KHATUN (1326-1416?) Daughter of the king of one of Shiraz's most turbulent times... Masud Shah; pupil and lifelong friend of the world's greatest mystical, lyric poet, Hafiz; the object of crazed desire by (among others) Iran's greatest satirist, the outrageous and visionary dervish poet Obeyd Zakani; lover, then wife of womanizer Amin al-Din, a minister of one of Persia's most loved, debauched and tragic rulers... Abu Ishak; imprisoned for twenty years under the Muzaffarids while her young daughter Soltan Bakht mysteriously died, possibly murdered. She was open-minded and scandalous and one of Iran's first feminists... this beautiful and sensuous, petite princess abdicated her royalty twice. She called herself 'a dervish maid' and is one of Iran's greatest poets whose *Divan* is four times larger than Hafiz's and contains 2000 *ghazals* and hundreds of *ruba'is* and *qita's* and a masterpiece *tarji-band* other forms of poetry.

Translations from...

Hafiz's Friend, Jahan Khatun: Persia's Princess Dervish Poet. A Selection of Poems from Her Divan. Translation Paul Smith and Rezvaneh Pashai. New Humanity Books 2006.

My dearest beloved, those wagging tongues told

you to stay away from your lover who's in decline.

Even if they want to execute you do not complain...

your thoughts and your actions to Mansur incline.

O breeze, when in the gardens please tell to my beloved,

"You are all that I desire... come, you to unification

take."

I'm joyful for my beloved comes, so tell my rival, "Leave!"

I will talk of beloved, or me like Mansur for execution

take.

*

NESIMI (1369-1417). Seyyid Ali Imadaddin Nesimi is considered one of the greatest mystical poets of the late 14th and early 15th centuries and one of the most prominent early masters in Turkish literary history.

Very little is known for certain about his life, including his real name. It is also possible that he was descended from the

Prophet Mohammed since he has sometimes been accorded the title of *seyyid* that is reserved for people claimed to be in Muhammad's line of descent. Nesimi's birthplace, like his real name, is wrapped in mystery: some claim that he was born in a province called Nesim, hence the pen-name. According to the Encyclopedia of Islam Nesimi was proficient also in Arabic and Persian and composed poems in both.

From his poetry, it's evident that Nesimi was greatly influenced by Mansur Hallaj and as a direct result of his beliefs that were considered blasphemous by contemporary religious authorities he was seized and according to most accounts... skinned alive in Aleppo.

A number of legends later grew up around his execution, such as the story that he mocked his executioners with improvised verse and, after the execution, draped his flayed skin around his shoulders and departed. His tomb in Aleppo remains an important place of pilgrimage to this day.

His work consists of two collections of poems, one of which, the rarer, is in Persian and the other in Turkish. The Turkish *Divan* consists of 250-300 *ghazals* and about 150 *ruba'is*. After his death his work continued to exercise a great influence on many Turkish language poets and authors.

Translations from...

Nesimi: Selected Poems, Translation & Introduction by Paul Smith, New Humanity Books, Campbells Creek, 2009.

"I am the Truth!" I cry, for like Mansur, the Truth helped

me!

I was this city's fortress so who wanted to on gibbet, me,

see?

I'm the Shrine of all that is true, the Beloved of the loving

devotees...

I'm Mansur of the worthy few and the heavenly *Kaaba*...

truthfully.

One drunk on Love in this world says, "I... am God!"

Mansur Hallaj is soon going to be hanging...

in intoxicated bliss.

This heart is manifested Light, Mt Sanai... our body:

our soul is like Moses that one can be seeing,

in intoxicated bliss.

If I should as Mansur once did, state: "I am God!"

Sir, I'm blameless, gallows taking breath away

I've found!

If you are fascinated like Moses by the face of God,

see yourself inside yourself and then this say:

"I've found!"

For that one's curls infamy Nesimi gave up fidelity:

you in dervish-coat, Christian hair-belt today

I've found!

Your form says, "I'm God!" I'll hang in Your curls noose.

One hung like Mansur, from love's noose isn't returning.

Show things of hypocrites are rosaries and prayer-mats...

Your perfumed curls shall into belts for Your, be turning.

O lover, if today with your Beloved you should be united

come here: like Nesimi this world with a kick be rejecting.

If for saying, "I am God" I'm hung, why should I be grieving?

Upon the gallows was not Mansur hung for all to see?

Come, see!

My heart's cut into pieces from grief due to parting from You:

Beloved, from my eye-wounds blood flows profusely...

come, see!

On this earth it's only the drunkards who leave a mark:

yes, Mansur was right... all life is lit up by love's spark.

O heart, the Truth... it lies in you, the Truth

is in you!

State the Truth, because: "I am the Truth...

is in you!

The Absolute Essence, the Absolute Truth

is in you!

Writing of the Book, by all true... in Truth,

is in you!

*

JAMI (Nov. 7, 1414- Nov. 9, 1492). Considered the last great poet of the Classical Period (9th-15th c.) Mulla Nur al-Din 'Abd al-Rahman ibn Ahmad Jami composed forty-three books but is mostly known for his seven *masnavis* epics greatly influenced by Nizami, including the best of them... *Joseph and Zulaikh* and *Layla and Majnun* and *Salman and Absal* and his mainly prose works *Lawa'ih: A Treatise on Sufism* and *The Beharistan (Abode of Spring)*. He also composed three *Divans* consisting of *ghazals, ruba'is, qasidas, qit'as* and other, mainly mystical, poems... he composed prefaces to each.

Translations from…

Jami: Selected Poems, Translation & Introduction by Paul; Smith,
New Humanity Books, Campbells Creek, 2008.

Try hard to keep the secret of your love to yourself:

because he told his, Mansur they were executing.

Jami, pearls from solitude's ocean are to be valued:

the self-absorbed ones aren't worth them receiving.

*

SA'IB (1601-1670). Mirza Muhammad Ali Tabrizi who used the *takhallus* of Sa'ib was born in Isfahan but he loved more the city of Tabriz, the birthplace of his parents where his father was a merchant who moved to Isfahan in the era of Shah Abbas the Great. He went to Mecca, then Kabul… where he was introduced to Shah Jahan. He went to Kashmir, then returned to Isfahan. His fame spread to India and Turkey mainly because he invented new styles of composing poetry, new concepts and philosophical and mystical and Sufi imagery.

Translation from…

The Divine Wine Volume Two, Translations & Introduction by
Paul Smith, New Humanity Books, Campbells Creek, 2005.

Love that inflames the world faith and infidelity

is beyond:

my neck the grip of Brahmin's thread and rosary

is beyond.

Mansur's jar of love was empty... so it made much noise,

or, in Unity's winehouse it of all to speak easily,

is beyond.

*

DARA SHIKOH (1615-1659). He was the oldest son of Emperor Shah Jahan and was known to be a loving husband, a good son and loving father. He was a fine poet, his poems having the influence of Sufism to which he was dedicated. He used 'Qadiri' as his *takhallus* or pen-name. His *Divan* of *ghazals, ruba'is* and *qasidas* in Persian was not the only work he left behind, his five prose works on Sufism and mysticism are popular in India even today. His *Majma al-Bahrain* or *The Mingling of the Two Oceans* is an explanation of the mystical sameness of Sufism and Vedanta. He also translated the *Upanishads, Bhagwad Gita and Yoga-Vasishta* into Persian.

He had a great breath of vision and was respected by many of the Sufi Masters of the time such as Shaikh Muhibbullah

Allabadi, Miyan Mir and Mulla Badakhshi and the 'naked' Sufi poet Sarmad (to follow). He was greatly loved by his niece Zeb-un-Nissa, the poetess 'Makhfi'.

After he was defeated after leading an uprising against his cruel, fundamentalist brother Emperor Aurangzeb, he was brutally killed on the 21st of August 1659.

Translation from...

Ruba'iyat of Dara Shikoh, Translation & introduction by Paul Smith, New Humanity Books, Campbells Creek, 2009.

Adam... mankind's father, Satan disowned,
didn't he?
Hallaj said, "I am the Truth" and got killed,
didn't he?
Really, it's the evil and malicious spirit of this priest...
every saint and every prophet he tormented,
didn't he?

*

MAKHFI (1639-1702). Princess Zeb-un-Nissa... (pen-name 'Makhfi') was the oldest daughter of the Mogul Emperor Aurungzeb of India. She revealed great intelligence from an early age and so received teaching. She discovered she had a remarkable memory and by the age of seven she had like Hafiz become a *hafiz*, one who had learnt the whole of the *Koran* by heart. Her proud father gave an enormous feast to celebrate, all his army in Delhi were feasted and the poor were given gold, businesses were closed for days.

A woman called Miyabai was hired as her teacher and in four years she had learnt Arabic, then mathematics and astronomy. She started to write a commentary on the *Koran* but her father objected and she had to stop. She had written poems from a young age in Arabic but a scholar from Arabia commented, "These are wise and clever poems and it is a miracle that a foreigner knows Arabic so well, but... it is still obvious that they were composed by an Indian." Being a perfectionist, from then on she only composed her poems in Persian.

At first she wrote her poetry in secret but her tutor, a scholar named Shah Rustom Ghazi, found her poems and prophesized her future greatness and went to her father and persuaded him to search India and Persia to find poets and bring them to come to Delhi to become a circle of poets surrounding her. She never married and was eventually imprisoned by her father for many years for being involved in a plot with her brother to unseat him and for her Sufi beliefs. She eventually died in prison.

Translation from…

Makhfi: The Princess Sufi Poet Zeb-un-Nissa, A selection of Poems from her Divan, Translation & Introduction by Paul Smith, New Humanity Books, Campbells Creek, 2006.

My body and soul thirst for Your Love and like Mansur every
grain of this body cries, "We are a part, You're all, we're
Divinity!"
Waves of Your Love's deluge roll over the boat of destruction…
soul drowned in love's depth a Noah could not lift to float
free.

*

BEDIL (1644-1721). Mirza Abdul-Qader Bedil is one of the most respected poets in Afghanistan. In the early 17th century, his family moved from Afghan Turkestan (Balkh region) to India, to live under the Moghul dynasty. Bedil himself, although ethnically an Uzbek, was born and educated in India, near Patna. In his later life he spent time travelling and visiting his ancestral lands. His writings in Persian are extensive. He was greatly influenced by Hafiz. His *Kulliyat* (complete works) consist of many *ghazals, rubai's, tarkib-bands, a tarjih-band, mu'ammas* (riddles) and more. He also wrote four *masnavis,* the most important being *Irfaan,* which he completed at age 68. It contains many stories and fairy tales, outlining his philosophical views. Bedil's 16 books of poetry contain nearly 147,000 couplets. With Ghalib he is considered a master of the complicated 'Indian Style' of *ghazal.*

Possibly as a result of being brought up in such a mixed religious environment, Bedil had considerably more tolerant views than his poetic contemporaries. He preferred free thought to accepting the established beliefs of his time, siding with the common people and rejecting the clergy who he often saw as corrupt. He essentially believed that the world was eternal, and in constant motion. He believed that all life was first mineral, then plant, then animal. He also expressed disbelief in judgement day and other orthodox tenets of faith. Despite this, he was by no means an atheist or a freethinker in the modern day sense. On the contrary, he had complicated views on the nature of God, heavily influenced by the Sufis (with whom he spent a considerable period of time).

Bedil enjoyed virtually no fame in Iran and only few scholars knew of him until recently. In Afghanistan and

Tajikistan however, he had a following that almost followed like a cult. People would get together at weekly Bedil meetings to study and interpret his poetry, and he was the poet of choice for many *ghazal* singers.

Translation from…

Unity in Diversity: Anthology of Sufi and Dervish Poets of the Indian-Subcontinent, Translation & Introduction by Paul Smith, New Humanity Books, Campbells Creek, 2003.

This feast of madness… so tender and beautiful,

it is;

uproar that creates a Resurrection, loud and full,

it is.

Into thinking of what Mansur said do not go too far:

every mosquito has its own echo… and powerful

it is!

*

RAHMAN BABA (1652-1711). Abdul Rahman (respectfully referred to as Rahman Baba) is considered by many to be the greatest Sufi Pashtun poet to compose poems, mainly *ghazals*, in the Pushtu language.

Rahman Baba was born in the early seventeenth century in the hilly Mohmand region of Afghanistan, outside of Peshwar. He was called 'The Nightingale of Peshwar'. This was a time when Afghanistan was under invasion by the Persians to the west and the Mongols to the east, a period of great struggle and hardship.

Yet, in the midst of this turmoil, the young Abdul Rahman showed himself to be an excellent student with a natural gift for poetry. But as he grew older he became disillusioned, questioning the real value of such pursuits. He withdrew from the world, becoming a hermit, dedicating himself to prayer and devotion. In his solitary worship... he wrote poetry, again.

Despite his reclusive life, Rahman Baba's poetry quickly spread and gained fame. Religious figures used his poetry to inspire the devout. Political leaders used his poems to inspire the independence movement. Rahman Baba's poetry became an important part of the nation's voice.

His *Divan* consists of 343 poems... *ghazals* and a few *qasidas.* Hafiz (many of Rahman's *ghazals* resemble his) and Sana'i were two major influences on him, but also the poems of Rumi, 'Iraqi and Jami.

Translation from...

Rahman Baba: Selected Poems, Translation & Introduction by Paul Smith, New Humanity Books Campbells Creek, 2009.

This, is the rose and that… is the thorn:

this is Mansur and the gallows-tree…

that is.

This is the beloved, that… malicious one:

this is the treasure, the viper, deadly…

that is.

*

KHWAJA MOHAMMAD (born mid-late 17th C.). The information on this poet is meagre. Little is known about him except that he lived in the reign of the fundamentalist Mughal emperor Aurangzeb and belonged to the Bangash tribe of Afghans who ruled the valley of that name and of which Kohatt is the chief town. Khwaja Mohammad lived the life of a dervish and followed the tenets of the Chishti sect. He was a disciple of Rahman Baba (above), who was a disciple of Mi'an Panju a celebrated Sufi Master who came originally from India and dwelt for many years in Afghanistan.

Khwaja Mohammad Bangash was a man of learning and passed most of his time with his teacher or spiritual guide. He is known to have performed the pilgrimage to Mecca and Medina and after his return he gave up writing poetry. His *Divan* is a very rare book. His *ghazals* in Pushtu are deeply mystical but occasionally he devotes a poem to the remembrance of lost friend.

Translation from…

Tongues on Fire: anthology of Sufi, Dervish, Warrior & court Poets of Afghanistan, Translation & Introduction by Paul Smith, New Humanity Books, Campbells Creek, 2006.

And love has brought scandal both in this world and the next:
on one named Majnun and on the son of Hallaj, named
Mansur.
And what would the hunter in the forest ever know about it,
if the partridge didn't signal him by calling so loud and
clear?

.

MUSHTAQ (1689-1758). Mir Sayyid Ali Mushtaq of Isfahan was in the literary movement that helped return poetry in the Persian language from the somewhat intricate and complex 'Indian Style'. He was influenced by Iraki, Sadi and Hafiz. It is said that he was the teacher of poetry of the traveller and author of the well-known biography of poets of the time and previous times *Atash-kada* (Fire Temple), Lutf 'Al Beg Adhar. Mushtaq was considered a master of the *ghazal* who brought new life into an old style and trained younger contemporaries besides Lutf and so influenced a whole generation. Many of his poems are mystical.

Translation from…

The Divine Wine, Volume Two, Translation & Introduction by Paul Smith, New Humanity Books, Campbells Creek, 2004.

> You, with a simple heart, who the Truth is speaking;
>
> you are like Mansur, all others are your foes… lying!
>
> A treasure is the Truth so when you find it, hide it…
>
> show it, you'll be responsible for your blood flowing!

OTHER BOOKS OF INTEREST PUBLISHED OR FORTHCOMING FROM NEW HUMANITY BOOKS

Most books are perfect-bound paperbacks 9" x 6" (23cm x 15cm), unless noted otherwise. Full colour miniatures on most covers.

Many of these books are available on KINDLE

TRANSLATIONS

(NOTE: All translations by Paul Smith are in clear, modern English and in the correct rhyme-structure of the originals and as close to the true meaning as possible.)

DIVAN OF HAFIZ
Revised Translation & Introduction by Paul Smith
This is a completely revised one volume edition of the only modern, poetic version of Hafiz's masterpiece of 791 *ghazals, masnavis, rubais* and other poems/songs. The spiritual and historical and human content is here in understandable, beautiful poetry: the correct rhyme-structure has been achieved, without intruding, in readable (and singable) English .
In the Introduction of 70 pages his life story is told in greater detail than any where else; his spirituality is explored, his influence on the life, poetry and art of the East and the West, the form and function of his poetry, and the use of his book as a worldly guide and spiritual oracle. His Book, like the *I Ching,* is one of the world's Great Oracles. Also included are notes to most of his poems, a glossary and selected bibliography and two indexes.
First published in a two-volume hardback limited edition in 1986 the book quickly went out of print. 557 pages.

PERSIAN AND HAFIZ SCHOLARS AND ACADEMICS WHO HAVE COMMENTED ON PAUL SMITH'S FIRST VERSION OF HAFIZ'S 'DIVAN'.
"It is not a joke... the English version of ALL the *ghazals* of Hafiz is a great feat and of paramount importance. I am astonished. If he comes to Iran I will kiss the fingertips that wrote such a masterpiece inspired by the Creator of all and I will lay down my head at his feet out of respect."
Dr. Mir Mohammad Taghavi (Dr. of Literature) Tehran.
"I have never seen such a good translation and I would like to write a book in Farsi and introduce his Introduction to Iranians." Mr B. Khorramshai, Academy of Philosophy, Tehran.

"Superb translations. 99% Hafiz 1% Paul Smith."
Ali Akbar Shapurzman, translator of many mystical works in English to
Persian and knower of Hafiz's *Divan* off by heart.
"I was very impressed with the beauty of these books." Dr. R.K. Barz.
Faculty of Asian Studies, Australian National University.
"Smith has probably put together the greatest collection of literary facts
and history concerning Hafiz." Daniel Ladinsky (Penguin Books author of
poems inspired by Hafiz).

HAFIZ – THE ORACLE (For Lovers, Seekers, Pilgrims, and the God-
Intoxicated).
Translation, Introduction & Interpretations by Paul Smith.
Hafiz's Divan has been used as an Oracle successfully by millions of
people from all walks of life for the past 600 years. The practice of
interpreting his poems has been going on in Iran for many centuries. Here
are almost four hundred of his *ghazals* with insightful and clear
interpretations by Paul Smith plus an Introduction that includes his life,
poetry, spirituality and the history of the use of his book as one of the
world's great Oracles. 438 pages

HAFIZ OF SHIRAZ.
The Life, Poetry and Times of the Immortal Persian Poet.
Three Volumes
by Paul Smith
Told through the eyes of Hafiz's lifelong friend and student Muhammad
Gulandam, This long, historical novel/biography of 1900 pages based on ten
years of research and writing covers Hafiz's life from age eight until after
his death. Shiraz is under siege by the tyrant Mubariz and Hafiz's friend
the king, Abu Ishak, is on the brink of madness and despair. Along the way
Hafiz falls in love with the beautiful Nabat, meets his Spiritual Master,
marries and had a son. He teaches at University and befriends the liberated
princess Jahan (Iran's greatest female poet) after being a student of the
outrageous poet/jester Obeyd Zakani. He experiences kingdoms rise and
fall, the people of his beloved city throw out dictators and the wrath of the
false Sufi and black magician Shaikh Ali Kolah. Mubariz takes control in
Shiraz closing the winehouses, imprisoning Hafiz's friend the poet, Princess
Jahan and forcing Obeyd Zakani to flee for his life. Abu Ishak is executed
and the false Sufi Ali Kolah is now in control of religious morals. Eventually
Mubariz's son Shah Shuja takes control but tragedy strikes Hafiz and
Jahan, and Nabat must suffer separation. Kingdoms rise and fall through
treachery and wars but through it all the songs/*ghazals* of Hafiz and his

minstrel friends help the brave Shirazis to carry on until finally Hafiz gives his Master Attar an ultimatum after 40 years of devotion... God-Realization or else! 2000 pages. 3 vols.

PIERCING PEARLS: THE COMPLETE ANTHOLOGY OF PERSIAN POETRY (Court, Sufi, Dervish, Satirical, Ribald, Prison & Social Poetry from the 9th to the 20th century.) Volume One
Translations, Introduction and Notes by Paul Smith
This 2 volume anthology is the largest anthology of Persian Poetry ever published.
The introduction contains a history and explanation of all the forms used by the poets, a short history of the Persian language, Sufism in Persian Poetry & a Glossary of Sufi & Dervish Symbols plus a Selected Bibliography. With each selection of a particular poet is a brief biography plus a list of further reading.
THE POETS... Volume One 9th to the 13th Century.
Abbas of Merv page 29, Hanzalah 30, Firuz 31, Abu Salik 32, Abu Shakur 33, Junaidi, 35, Shahid, 36, Rudaki 38, Agachi 48, Rabi'a Balkhi 49, Khusravani 57, Manjik 58, Daqiqi 60, Mantiki 67, Umarah 69, Kisa'i 70, Firdausi 74, Baba Tahir 83, Farrukhi 88, Asjadi 100, Manuchirhri 101, Gurgani 106, Unsuri 110, Abu Said 116, Ibn Sina 123, Baba Kuhi 125, Nasir-i-Khusraw 127, Asadi 131, Azraqi 137, Qatran 140, Ansari 145, Al-Ghazali 147, Mas'ud Sad 149, Mu'izzi 159, Hamadani 168, Omar Khayyam 172, Sana'i 174, Sabir 189, Mahsati 182, Jabali 193, Vatvat 197, Anvari 201, Falaki 212, Khaqani 229, Zahir 242, Nizami 252, Ruzbihan 286, Baghdadi 288, 'Attar 290, Auhad ud-din Kermani 315, Kamal ad-din 320, Hamavi 325, Baba Afzal 328, Rumi 331, Imami 389, Hamgar 390, Sadi 395, Iraki 439, Humam 452, Amir Khusraw 457, Hasan Dilhavi 473, Simnani 475, Auhadi 478, Ibn Yamin 484, Khaju 490. Pages... 510

PIERCING PEARLS: THE COMPLETE ANTHOLOGY OF PERSIAN POETRY (Court, Sufi, Dervish, Satirical, Ribald, Prison & Social Poetry from the 9th to the 20th century.) Volume Two
Translations, Introduction and Notes by Paul Smith
This 2 volume anthology is the largest anthology of Persian Poetry ever published.
The introduction contains a history and explanation of all the forms used by the poets, a short history of the Persian language, Sufism in Persian Poetry & a Glossary of Sufi & Dervish Symbols plus a Selected Bibliography. Included with each selection of a particular poet is a brief biography plus a list of further reading.

THE POETS: Volume Two... 14th Century to Modern Times
Obeyd Zakani page 27, Emad 63, Salman 76, Shahin 84, Hafiz 105, Ruh
Attar 173, Haydar 189, Azad 203, Junaid Shirazi 206, Jahan Khatun 211,
Shah Shuja 244, Kamal 249, Maghribi 253, Bushaq 263, Kasim Anwar 276,
Shah Ni'tmu'llah 284, Jami 291, Fighani 309, Babur 314, Humayan 317,
Kamran 319, Ghazali 321, Kahi 323, Akbar 325, Urfi 326, Hayati 331, Ulfati
332, Dara Shikoh 333, Sarmad 336, Sa'ib 343, Nasir Ali 347, Makhfi 348,
Bedil 358, Mushtaq 366, Hatif 370, Tahirah 377, Iqbal 392, Parvin 398, Khalili
423, Rahi 426, Simin 428, Nurbaksh 430. Pages 444.

DIVAN OF SADI: His Mystical Love-Poetry.
Translation & Introduction by Paul Smith
Sadi's mystical love poetry, his *ghazals,* although almost unknown in the
West, are loved by his fellow-countrymen almost as much as those of Hafiz
whom he greatly influenced. Here for the first time in English they can be
read in all their beauty and power and spirit.
ALL of the wonderful 603 *ghazals* from Sadi's *Badayi* and *Tayyibat* have
been translated in clear, modern, meaningful, correct-rhyming English.
Included is an Introduction containing The Life of Sadi, his Poetry and his
influence on the East and the West and on the form and meaning of the
ghazal. 406 pages.

RUBA'IYAT OF SADI
Translation & Introduction by Paul Smith
Here for the first time in beautiful English are eighty-eight of Sadi's
wonderful short poems or *ruba'is* in the correct rhyme-structure and with all
the meanings. Some are mystical others romantic, some satirical and
humourous and others critical of the selfishness of the time, of all time. As
fresh today as they were when they were composed some 800 years ago.
Included is an Introduction containing The Life of Sadi, his Poetry and his
influence on the East and the West and a history of the form of the *ruba'i*
and examples by its greatest exponents. 132 pages.

WINE, BLOOD & ROSES: ANTHOLOGY OF TURKISH POETS
Sufi, Dervish, Divan, Court & Folk Poetry from the 14th – 20th Century
Translations, Introductions, Notes etc., by Paul Smith
Introduction includes chapters on...The Turkish Language, Turkish Poetry,
The Ghazal in Turkish Poetry, The Roba'i in Turkish Poetry, The Mesnevi
in Turkish Poetry, The Qasida in Turkish Poetry and a Glossary.
Included with each selection of a particular poet is a brief biography plus a
list of further reading.

OBEYD ZAKANI: THE DERVISH JOKER.
A Selection of his Poetry, Prose, Satire, Jokes and Ribaldry.
Translation & Introduction by Paul Smith

Obeyd Zakani is an important a figure in Persian and Sufi literature and poetry. His satire, humorous stories, ribald and obscene poems, social commentary, mystical *ghazals*, prose, *ruba'is* and his famous epic *qasida* 'Mouse & Cat' are popular today and are more relevant than ever.

He is considered to be one of the world's greatest satirist and social-commentator whose life and mystical poems had a great influence on his student and friend Hafiz and many others.

This is by far the largest selection of his work available in the English language. 286 pages.

OBEYD ZAKANI'S > MOUSE & CAT ^ ^
(The Ultimate Edition)
Translation & Introduction etc by Paul Smith

Obeyd Zakani's *Mouse & Cat* is a satirical, epic fable in the poetic form of the *qasida* that was influential at the time it was composed (14th C.) and has remained so for the past 600 years. It is more than just a story for children (that some say brought about the cartoon of Tom & Jerry)… it is a story of the stupidity of the false power of those in power and a warning to all that such blind ambition always leads to destruction at the hands of one even more powerful.

Here is a beautiful, poetic translation keeping to the correct form of the famous *qasida* illustrated with unique Persian miniatures.

Included is a long Introduction on The Life, Times and Writings of Obeyd Zakani.

Appendixes include… Examples of all other translations into English; Obeyd performs *Mouse & Cat* for a young prince (from the Novel/Biog. *Hafiz of Shiraz*); a 1940's Illustrated Persian edition of *Mouse & Cat*, The Corrected Persian Text of *Mouse & Cat* and The First Complete Translation into literal English in 1906. Selected Bibliography. 169 pages.

THE GHAZAL: A WORLD ANTHOLOGY
Translations, Introductions, Notes, Etc. by Paul Smith

Introduction includes...TheGhazal in Arabic, Persian, Turkish, Urdu, Punjabi, Pushtu, Sindhi, Kashmiri & English Poetry. Glossary.
Included with each selection of a particular poet is a brief biography plus a list of further reading.

THE POETS...Hazrat Ali page 27, Rabi'a of Basra 28, Dhu'l-Nun 32, Mansur al-Hallaj 34, Khusravani 37, Shahid 38, Manjik 39, Rudaki 40, Rabi'a Balkhi 43, Daqiqi 47, Kisa'i 49, Firdausi 51, Unsuri 53, Baba Kuhi 56, Qatran 57, Mas'ud Sa'd 59, Mu'izzi 62, Sana'i 64, Sabir 67, Falaki 69, Jabali 72, Vatvat 74, Anvari 75, Khaqani 77, Nizami 80, 'Attar 84, Kamal ud-din 96, Ibn al-Farid 98, Ibn 'Arabi 101, Rumi 106, Imami 121, Sadi 122, Hamgar 154, Iraki 156, Humam 163, Yunus Emre 165, Amir Khusraw 177, Hasan Dilhavi 188, Auhadi 190, Ibn Yamin 192, Khaju 193, Obeyd Zakani 199, Emad 208, Salman 218, Azad 221, Hafiz 224, Ruh Attar 264, Haydar 269, Junaid Shirazi 274, Kadi Burhan-ud-din 278, Jahan Khatun 281, Kamal 302, Maghribi 305, Nesimi 314, Bushaq 325, Shah Ni'matu'llah 337, Ahmedi 339, Sheykhi 343, Kasim Anwar 345, Jami 350, Baba Fighani 363, Babur 368, Ahmed Pasha 370, Mihri 372, Zeyneb 377, Jem 379, Necati 382, Zati 386, Pir Sultan 390, Khayali 394, Kamran 401, Fuzuli 402, Huda'i 412, Kahi 414, Baqi 416, Urfi 422, Yahya 425, Qutub Shah 428, Mirza 431, Haleti 442, Sa'ib 444. Na'ili 446, Niyazi 449. Khushal 452, Ashraf Khan 467, Makhfi 473, Nabi 507, Bedil 510, Abdul-Khadir 514, Rahman Baba 521, Khwaja Mohammad 536, Hamid 547, Wali 557, Nedim 561, Mushtaq 565, Ali Haider 567, Fitnet 568, Sauda 573, Dard 575, Ahmad Shah 578, Shaida 486, Nazir 592, Mir 599, Sachal Sarmast 606, Galib 611, Esrar Dede 618, Lelya Khanim 620, Mahmud Gami 621, Aatish 623, Zauq 627, Ghalib 630, Momin 636, Tahirah 639, Shad 647, Iqbal 651, Ashgar 657, Mahjoor 660, Jigar 613, Huma 669, Veysel 695, Firaq 699, Josh 704, Parvin 707, Rahi 713, Faiz 715, Simin 717, Paul 719. Pages 745.

NIZAMI: THE TREASURY OF MYSTERIES
Translation & Introduction by Paul Smith

"The Makhzanol Asrar (The Treasury of Mysteries), the most beautiful mystic poem in the Persian language, has both perfection of language and grandeur of thought. Every line of his Treasury of Mysteries is a living witness to his absolute certainty that piety, devotion, humility and self-forgetfulness are the corner stones of total annihilation, which in turn is necessary for unification with God and the foundation of the edifice of eternal life." G. H. Darab. Senior lecturer in Persian. University of London. Translator of Nizami.

Paul Smith has kept to the correct rhyme-structure while retaining the meaning and beauty of the original in simple, understandable, poetic English. He has written a long Introduction on the Life of Nizami and chapters on each of his books of poetry. Selected Bibliography. 236 pages.

NIZAMI: LAYLA AND MAJNUN
Translation & Introduction by Paul Smith
It is impossible to underestimate the effect of Nizami's 'Layla and Majnun' on the world over the past 800 years. Many poets throughout this period have copied or been influenced by his story of the young lovers. Many Master-Poets besides Ibn Arabi, Attar, Rumi, Sadi, Hafiz and Jami have quoted from him or like him have used the story of the desperate lovers to illustrate how human love can be transformed into divine love through separation and longing. It is said that no one has painted a more perfect picture of women in Persian Literature than Nizami.
Paul Smith has kept to the correct rhyme-structure of this long *masnavi* epic poem, while retaining the beauty of the poetry, the mystical meaning and simplicity of the form. He has included a long Introduction on his life and chapters on all of the works of this great Master/Poet. Selected Bibliography. 236 pages.

RUBA'IYAT OF RUMI
Translation & Introduction and Notes by Paul Smith
Here are 330 wonderful *ruba'is* of the great Spiritual Master of the 13th century, who has become today the most popular poet in the world, Jelal ad-din Rumi: they are powerful, spiritual and full of joy, bliss and understanding. Unlike those of Omar Khayyam's these are poems composed by a soul before and *after* gaining God-realisation.
Included in the Introduction is the life of Rumi and a history of the *ruba'i* and examples by its greatest exponents. Selected Bibliography.
The correct rhyme-structure has been kept as well as the beauty and meaning of these immortal four-line poems. 370 pages.

RUMI: SELECTED POEMS
Translation, Introduction & Notes by Paul Smith
Included in the Introduction is the life of Rumi and chapters on the *ruba'i,* the *ghazal,* the *masnavi and the qasida.* Selected Bibliography. Glossary.
The correct rhyme-structure has been kept as well as the beauty and meaning of these immortal poems of this most popular Perfect Spiritual Master and Master Poet. 199 pages.

THE MASNAVI: A WORLD ANTHOLOGY
Translations, Introduction and Notes by Paul Smith
Introduction includes… Article on the masnavi in various languages.
With each selection of a particular poet is a brief biography plus a list of
further reading.
THE POETS…Abu Shakur page 13, Rabi'a Balkhi 15, Daqiqi 21, Firdausi
26, Gurgani 35, Nasir-i-Khusraw 39, Asadi 43, Sana'i 44, Khaqani 49,
Zahir 52, Nizami 55, 'Attar 83, Rumi 91, Sadi 128, Sultan Valad 135, Yunus
Emre 140, Amir Khusraw 144, Auhadi 149, Khaju 152, Obeyd Zakani 152,
Shahin 157, Hafiz 178, Ruh Attar 192, Kasim Anwar 196, Shah Ni'tmu'llah
200, Jami 207, Fuzuli 207, Mir 210, Tahirah 219, Iqbal 225, Inayat Khan 231,
Parvin 248, Paul 257. 268 pages.

HAFIZ'S FRIEND, JAHAN KHATUN: The Persian Princess
Dervish Poet…A Selection of Poems from her *Divan*
Translated by Paul Smith and Rezvaneh Pashai.
Daughter of the king of one of Shiraz's most turbulent times (8th century
A.H. 14th century A.D.) … Masud Shah; pupil and lifelong friend of the
world's greatest mystical, lyric poet, Hafiz of Shiraz; the object of crazed
desire by (among others) Iran's greatest satirist, the obscene, outrageous,
visionary poet Obeyd Zakani; lover, then wife of womaniser Amin al-Din,
a minister of one of Persia's most loved, debauched and tragic rulers Abu
Ishak; imprisoned for twenty years under the Muzaffarids while her young
daughter mysteriously died; open-minded and scandalous, one of Iran's first
feminists … the beautiful, petite princess who abdicated her royalty twice;
one of Iran's greatest classical lyric poets; a prolific, profound, infamous
female Persian poet… one of the greatest mystical love poets of all time
whose *Divan* is four times the size of Hafiz's. 183 pages.

KABIR: SEVEN HUNDRED SAYINGS (SAKHIS).
Translation & Introduction by Paul Smith
'Here are wonderful words of wisdom from one of the wisest of the wise.
Here are lines of love from a Master of Divine Love, and a human being
who has lived as all human beings should live, with compassion, honesty
and courage. If you want the Truth, no holds barred, it is here, but as we're
told; truth is dangerous! These poems change people. You will not be the
same! As Kabir says. "Wake up sleepy head!" ' From the Introduction
which includes a Glossary & Selected Bibliography. 188 pages.

PRINCESSES, SUFIS, DERVISHES, MARTYRS & FEMINISTS: NINE GREAT WOMEN POETS OF THE EAST

A Selection of the Poetry of Rabi'a of Basra, Rabi'a of Balkh, Mahsati, Lalla Ded, Jahan Khatun, Makhfi, Tahirah, Hayati and Parvin.

Introduction & Translations by Paul Smith

Rabi'a of Basra (d. 801) is considered one of the greatest Saints and founders of Sufism and composed powerful spiritual verse in Arabic.

Rabi'a of Balkh (10th c.) was the princess of Afghanistan whose love for a slave of her father the king caused her downfall at the hands of her mad brother… she wrote many of her poems to her beloved in her own blood on the walls of the prison where he tortured her to death.

Mahsati (12th century) was the liberated court poet of Sultan Sanjar who knew Nizami, Omar Khayyam and other poets of that time. Like Omar she only composed in the *ruba'i* form that she revolutionized with her often scandalous verse.

Lalla Ded (1320-1392) is the famous female poet/saint from Kashmir who lived at *exactly* the same time as Hafiz of Shiraz (1320-1392). Her *vakhs* (poem/sayings) are sung even today in Kashmir. She was married at a young age but the marriage was a failure and she walked out at the age of twenty-four. It must have taken a lot of courage on her part to walk around unclothed as she did. She was treated with contempt by some and much reverence by others, seeing her as a saint and eventually as God-realized. Her two hundred *vakhs* are some of the oldest examples of Kashmiri written. She was a bridge between Hindu mysticism and Sufism.

Jahan Khatun (1326-1416) was a beautiful, liberated princess in Shiraz and a friend and pupil of the great Hafiz… her *Divan* is four times the size of his. She spent 20 years in prison where her daughter died. Her *ghazals, ruba'is* and other fine poems put her in the highest rung of Persian Poets.

Makhfi or *Zebunissa* (1638-1702) was the daughter of the fundamentalistmperor of India Aurangzeb and was eventually imprisoned by him and tortured to death for her Sufi views and conspiring with a brother to overthrow him. Her over 550 *ghazals* and *ruba'is* in classical Persian are deep, powerful, spiritual and at times heartbreaking.

Tahirah…(1817-1853). Tahirah was a beautiful and intelligent woman who led a short and stormy life. She became a devotee of the Bab, who from Shiraz had given his prophetic message that would later appear in the form of Baha-ul-lah, the founder of the Baha'is. She was not only a poet but also wrote prose, knew literature, religious laws and interpretations of the *Koran* and lectured… very unusual for a woman of that time and previous times in Iran. She was thirty-six when sentenced to death after the Shah was assassinated leading to a massacre of the Baha'is.

Hayati (mid 18th century - early 19th century). Bibi Hayati Kermani was born into a Sufi family in the Kerman province of Persia. She was raised by her brother, who guided her in the early stages of her spiritual life. When she was older she was initiated into the Ni'matullahi Sufi order by the Sufi Master Nur 'Ali Shah, who she was later to marry. At the request of her husband Hayati quickly composed her poetry and in her lifetime became well-known for her passionate, mystical poems that combine her great love for her husband with her devotion to Hazrat 'Ali and union with God. *Parvin...*(1907-1941). Parvin E'tesami was one of Iran's greatest female poets. She learned Arabic and Persian literature from her father. She composed her first poems at eight and knew most Iranian poets by the time she was eleven, having a remarkable memory. She received a Medal of Art and Culture in 1936. Her poems had mainly social or mystical subjects, often being about the tyranny of the rich and the rights of the poor and the downtrodden and the role of women. She died in 1941 from Typhoid. The correct rhyme-structure has been kept as well as the beauty and meaning of these beautiful, sometimes mystical poems. Pages 367.

SHAH LATIF: SELECTED POEMS
Translation & Introduction by Paul Smith
Shah Abdul Latif (1689-1752) was a Sufi Master and is considered by many to be the greatest poet of the Sindhi language. His book of poetry is called the *Risalo.* His shrine is located in Bhit and attracts hundreds of pilgrims every day. He is the most famous Sindhi poet and Sufi. He was not just adored for poetry, people from far and near respected and loved him as a Spiritual Master. He composed *dohas* (self-contained strict-rhyming couplets popular with poet-saints of India like Kabir, Surdas, Tukaram) and freed it from the chain of two lines, extending it to even five or six couplets, often with irregular rhyme structures. He also introduced one more string to the *tambura,* a drone instrument and founded a new tradition in music based on the synthesis of high art and folk art. He told the basic principles of Sufism in his poetry, often using folktales about human love such as that of Sasui and Punhu, becoming a bridge to Divine Love. 172 pages

LALLA DED: SELECTED POEMS
Translation & Introduction by Paul Smith
Lalla Ded is the famous female poet/saint from Kashmir who lived at *exactly* the same time as Hafiz of Shiraz (1320-1392). Her *vakhs* (poem/sayings) are sung even today in Kashmir. She was married at a young age but the marriage was a failure and she walked out at the age of twenty-four. She became a disciple of Siddha Srikanth. It must have taken a lot of

courage on her part to walk out of a marriage and to walk around unclothed as she did. She was treated with contempt by some and much reverence by others, seeing her as a saint and eventually as God-realized. Her two hundred *vakhs* are some of the oldest examples of Kashmiri written. She was a bridge between Hindu mysticism and Sufism. Her poems are more influential today than ever, not only in Kashmir but around the world. Here are 134 poems with correct form and meaning. 140 pages.

BULLEH SHAH: SELECTED POEMS
Translation & Introduction by Paul Smith
Bulleh Shah (1680-1758) was a Sufi poet who composed in Punjabi and settled in Kasur, now in Pakistan. His Spiritual Master was Shah Inayat. The poetic form Bulleh Shah is called the *Kafi*, a style of Punjabi poetry used not only by the Sufis of Sindh and Punjab, but also by Sikh gurus. His poetry and philosophy strongly criticizes the Islamic religious orthodoxy of his day. His time was marked with communal strife between Muslims and Sikhs. But in that age Bulleh Shah was a beacon of hope and peace for the citizens of Punjab. Several of his songs or *kafis* are regarded as an integral part of the traditional repertoire of *qawwali,* the musical genre that represents the devotional music of the Sufis. The correct rhyme-structure has been kept as well as the beauty and meaning of these poems. 141 pages.

NIZAMI: MAXIMS
Translation & Introduction Paul Smith
Nizami (d. 1208) is a true Sufi Master Poet who is most famous for his six books in *masnavi* form: *The Treasury of the Mysteries, Layla and Majnun, Khrosrau and Shirin, The Seven Portraits* and his two books on Alexander. He also composed a *Divan* of approximately 20,000 couplets mostly in *ghazals* and *ruba'is...* tragically only 200 couplets survive. His influence on Attar, Rumi, Sadi, Hafiz, Jami, Shakespeare and others that followed was profound. Included in the Introduction... on the Life, Times & Poetry of Nizami includes chapters on his six *masnavis* and his *Divan,* and on the various forms of poetry he used and a Selected Bibliography. The correct rhyme-structure has been kept as well as the beauty and meaning of these wonderful two-line maxims that are not only profound, but also simple. Illustrated 214 pages.

KHIDR IN SUFI POETRY: A SELECTION
Translation & Introduction by Paul Smith
Khidr (Khizer, Khadir) is often called: "The Green One" for he was said to have drunk from the Fountain of Immortality and gained Eternal life. He

has been identified with Elias, St. George, Phineas, the Angel Gabriel, the companion of Mohammed on a journey which is told in the *Koran, viii,* 59-8 1, and throughout the literature of Mysticism has appeared to many great seekers who eventually became Perfect Masters. Here are poems by many great Sufi Master Poets who have composed poems in Persian, Turkish, Pashtu, Urdu and English in which he is invoked or appears: Ansari, Anvari, Khaqani, Mu'in, Nizami, 'Attar, Baba Afzal, Rumi, Sadi, Yunus Emre, Shabistari, Amir Khusrau, Obeyd Zakani, Emad Kermani, Hafiz, Ruh Attar, Haydar, Jahan Khatun, Ahmedi, Zeyneb, Necati, Khushal, Makhfi, Rahman Baba, Khwaja Mohammad, Niyazi, Wali, Dard, Zauq, Ghalib, Dagh, Iqbal, Paul. The correct rhyme-structure has been kept as well as the beauty and meaning of these poems in various forms. Introduction on 'Who is Khidr'... Three Appendixes. Illustrated. 267 pages.

ADAM: THE FIRST PERFECT MASTER AND POET
by Paul Smith

In a series of conversations between a Master and devotees over a number of days and nights this is a long-overdue exploration and discovery and appreciation of the real spiritual status of Adam, the first God-realized human being and the first poet. Using poetry and texts of the greatest Sufi and other mystical poets this first Perfect Master's life and role is revealed and praised. The poets and Spiritual Masters include Adam Himself, Hafiz, Ibn 'Arabi, Shahin of Shiraz, 'Iraqi, Jili, Hallaj, Khushal Khan Khattak, Rumi, Ansari, Nizami, Surawadi, Mu'in ud-din Chishti, Sadi, Ibn al-Farid and Paul. The correct rhyme-structure has been kept as well as the beauty and meaning of these poems in various forms. 185 pages.

MODERN SUFI POETRY: A SELECTION
Translations & Introduction by Paul Smith

Here is one of the few anthologies of modern Sufi poetry of poets that have made a lasting impression on the present times. All the poets and Poet/Masters in this collection either died or were born in the 20th century. Most of the poets in this collection composed in the forms of earlier Sufi poets: *ghazal, ruba'i, qasida, kafi, masnavi.* Introduction: Sufis & Dervishes: Their Art and Use of Poetry, The Main Forms in Sufi and Dervish Poetry. THE POETS: Hali 47, Farid 51, Shad 57, Khusrawi 66, Iqbal 70, Munis 'Ali Shah 90, Inayat Khan 97, Asghar 122, Jigar 128, Khadim 140, Huma 151, Veysel 168, Firaq 175, Josh 185, Francis Brabazon 194, Khalili 207, Nurbaksh 214, Paul 217. Pages 249

LIFE, TIMES & POETRY OF NIZAMI
Paul Smith

Nizami (d. 1208) is a true Sufi Master Poet who is most famous for his six books in *masnavi* form: *The Treasury of the Mysteries, Layla and Majnun, Khrosrau and Shirin, The Seven Portraits* and his two books on Alexander. He also composed a *Divan* of approximately 20,000 couplets mostly in *ghazals* and *ruba'is*... tragically only 200 couplets survive. His influence on Attar, Rumi, Sadi, Hafiz and Jami and all others that followed was profound. Here a number of his *ghazals* and *ruba'is* and a *qasida* translated into English and a good selection from his *masnavis*. This book is on The Life and Times and Poetry of Nizami and on the various forms of poetry he used and the reason why he composed his major works and their effect on the times and our time. Selected Bibliography. The correct rhyme-structure has been kept as well as the beauty and meaning of the selected beautiful, mystical poems. 97 pages.

RABI'A OF BASRA: SELECTED POEMS
Translation by Paul Smith

RABI'A OF BASRA (717-801). Throughout her life, her Love of God, poverty and self-denial did not waver. She did not possess much other than a broken jug, a rush mat and a brick, which she used as a pillow. She spent nights in prayer and contemplation, chiding herself if she slept because it took her away from her active Love of God. As her fame grew she had many disciples. More interesting than her asceticism is the actual concept of Divine Love that Rabi'a introduced. She was the first to introduce the idea that God should be loved for God's own sake, not out of fear -- as earlier Sufis had done. She taught that repentance was a gift from God as none could repent unless God had already accepted him and given this gift of repentance. She had a high ideal, worshipping God neither from fear of Hell nor from hope of Paradise, for she saw such self-interest as unworthy of God's servants; emotions like fear and hope were like veils. She is widely considered the most important of the early Sufi poets. Here are most of the small number of her poems that survive, in the forms in which they were composed, also an introduction on her life and times and a chapter on Sufi poetry. 100 pages.

SATIRICAL PROSE OF OBEYD ZAKANI
Translation and Introduction by Paul Smith

Obeyd Zakani is an important a figure in Persian and Sufi literature and poetry. His satire, humorous stories, ribald and obscene poems, social commentary, mystical *ghazals*, prose, *ruba'is* and his famous epic *qasida*

'Mouse & Cat' are popular today and are more relevant than ever. He is considered to be one of the world's greatest satirist and social-commentator whose life and mystical poems had a great influence on his student and friend Hafiz and many others. Here are most of his hilarious and often obscene satirical prose works, mostly fully translated... Including his *Definitions, Joyous Treatise, The Ethics of the Nobles, The Book of the Beard* and *A Hundred Maxims*. Included is a long Introduction on his Life & Times in Shiraz and his relationship to Hafiz and the princess poet, Jahan Khatun. Selected Bibliography. 212 pages

KHAQANI: SELECTED POEMS
Translation & Introduction by Paul Smith
Born in Shirwan in 1122 he died in Tabriz in 1199. He was a great poet and a master of the *qasida* and one of the first of the *ghazal*. He was born into the family of a carpenter in Melgem, near Shamakhy. He lost his father and was brought up by an uncle, a doctor and astronomer at court of the Shirwanshah, who acted 'as his nurse and tutor'. His mother was a Christian and Jesus features in many of his poems. After he was invited to court he assumed the pen-name Khaqani ('regal'). A court poet's life bored him and he fled to Iraq inspiring his famous *masnavi* 'A Gift from the Two Iraqs'. He also wrote 'The Ruin of Madain' painting his impression of the remains of Sassanid's Palace near the Ctesiphon. Returning home Shah Akhistan ordered his imprisonment. Released he moved to Tabriz but his small son died, then daughter, then wife. Alone, he soon died. He is buried at the Poet's Cemetery in Tabriz. He left a remarkable, large heritage of poems in Persian that influenced many 'court' and Sufi poets. A major influence on his poems was Sana'i. Introduction on his Life, Poetry & Times and Forms he composed in. The correct rhyme-structure has been kept in this largest selection of his poems including *ruba'is, ghazals, masnavi, qasidas, qit'as* in English. Selected Bibliography. 195 pages.

IBN 'ARABI: SELECTED POEMS
Translation & Introduction by Paul Smith
In the West he is known as the *Doctor Maximus* and in the Islamic world as *The Great Master*. Born in Murcia in Spain in 1165 his family moved to Seville. At thirty-five he left for Mecca where he completed his most influential book of poems *The Interpreter of Ardent Desires* and began writing his masterpiece, the vast *Meccan Revelations*. In 1204 he began further travels. In 1223 he settled in Damascus where he lived the last seventeen years of his life, being executed in 1240. His tomb there is still an important place of pilgrimage. A prolific writer, Ibn 'Arabi is generally

known as the prime exponent of the idea later known as the 'Unity of Being'. His emphasis was on the true potential of the human being and the path to realizing that potential and becoming the Perfect or complete person. Hundreds of works are attributed to him including a large *Divan* of poems most of which have yet to be translated. Introduction on his life and poetry. The correct rhyme-structure has been kept as well as the beauty and meaning of this selection of his beautiful, mystical poems. 121 pages.

RIBALD POEMS OF THE SUFI POETS
Sana'i, Anvari, Mahsati, Rumi, Sadi, Obeyd Zakani
Translations, Introductions Paul Smith
Some of the greatest of the Persian Sufi poets composed ribald and at times 'obscene' poems for satirical and often (as in the case of Rumi) for teaching some spiritual truth or moral. Here is a wide-ranging selection of the greatest of them from the eleventh to the fourteenth century. Here are at times hilarious, witty, weird, and erotic and obscene poems in most of the various forms of classical Persian poetry… the *ghazal,* the *ruba'i,* the *masnavi,* the *qit'a,* the *qasida* and the *tarji-band.* 190 pages.

THE GHAZAL IN SUFI & DERVISH POETRY: An Anthology
Translations, Introductions, Etc. by Paul Smith
Introduction includes: The *Ghazal* in Arabic, Persian, Turkish, Urdu, Punjabi, Sindhi, Pushtu, Kashmiri & English Sufi & Dervish Poetry; Sufis & Dervishes: Their Art and Use of Poetry. Glossary of Sufi Symbols.
Included with each selection of a particular poet is a brief biography plus a list of further reading.
THE POETS… Hazrat Ali page 33, Rabi'a of Basra 34, Dhu'l-Nun 38, Mansur al-Hallaj 40, Rudaki 42, Baba Kuhi 44, Sana'i 45, Khaqani 48, Nizami 50, 'Attar 54, Kamal ud-din 65, Ibn al-Farid 66, Ibn 'Arabi 69, Rumi 74, Imami 88, Sadi 69, Iraki 118, Humam 125, Yunus Emre 127, Amir Khusraw 138, Hasan Dihlavi 148, Auhadi 150, Ibn Yamin 152, Khaju 153, Obeyd Zakani 158, Emad 167, Hafiz 176, Ruh Attar 213, Ahmedi 218, Haydar 222, Junaid Shirazi 226, Kadi Burhan-ud-din 230, Jahan Khatun 233, Kamal 252, Maghribi 255, Nesimi 264, Sheykhi 273, Kasim Anwar 276, Shah Ni'matu'llah 280, Jami 281, Baba Fighani 293, Pir Sultan 298, Khayali 302, Fuzuli 308, Huda'i 317, Qutub Shah 325, Mirza 327, Sa'ib 337, Khushal 340, Ashraf Khan 349, Makhfi 354, Bedil 385, Abdul-Khadir 389, Rahman Baba 395, Khwaja Mohammad 409, Hamid 419, Niyazi 428, Wali 430, Mushtaq 434, Ali Haider 436, Sauda 437, Dard 439, Nazir 455, Mir 462, Sachal Sarmast 468, Galib 473, Esrar Dede 479, Aatish 481, Zauq 484, Tahirah

487, Shad 491, Iqbal 495, Ashgar 500, Jigar 503, Huma 508, Veysel 532, Paul 536. Pages 560.

MAKHFI: THE PRINCESS SUFI POET ZEB-UN-NISSA
A Selection of Poems from her *Divan*
Translation & Introduction by Paul Smith
Makhfi (1638-1702) pen-name meaning 'concealed', was Zeb-un-Nissa the beautiful and talented oldest daughter of the strict Muslim Emperor of India, Aurangzeb. She was imprisoned for 20 years for her Sufi views and conspiring with a brother against him. Her over 550 *ghazals* and *ruba'is* in Persian are deep, spiritual and at times truly heartbreaking.
The correct forms and spiritual meaning are preserved in this large selection of her poetry. Selected Bibliography. 120 pages.

~THE SUFI RUBA'IYAT~ A Treasury of Sufi and Dervish Poetry
in the Ruba'i form, from Rudaki to the 21st Century
Translations, Introductions, Notes etc. by Paul Smith
Introduction includes…Sufis & Dervishes: Their Art and Use of Poetry… The Form of the Ruba'i in Persian, Arabic, Turkish, Urdu & English Sufi & Dervish Poetry & a Glossary.
Included with each selection of a particular poet is a brief biography plus a list of further reading.
THE POETS…Rudaki page 31, Mansur al-Hallaj 34, Shibli 36, Baba Tahir 37, Abu Said 42, Ibn Sina 48, Baba Kuhi 51, Ansari 52, Al-Ghazzali 54, Hamadani 56, Sana'i 58, Mahsati 62, Khaqani 66, Nizami 70, Ruzbihan 72, Baghdadi 74, 'Attar 76, Auhad-ud-din Kermani 83, Kamal ud-din 87, Hamavi 91, Baba Afzal 93, Rumi 96, Imami 106, Sadi 107, Iraki 112, Sultan Valad 117, Humam 119, Amir Khusraw 121, Simnani 125, Ibn Yamin 127, Khaju 128, Obeyd Zakani 130, Emad 132, Hafiz 133, Ruh Attar 141, Kadi Burhan-ud-din 142, Jahan Khatun 144, Kamal 152, Maghribi 152, Nesimi 155, Kasim Anwar 158, Shah Ni'matu'llah 159, Jami 162, Baba Fighani 165, Fuzuli 166, Ghazali 168, Urfi 170, Qutub Shah 172, Haleti 174, Dara Shikoh 176, Sarmad 179, Sa'ib 189, Nasir Ali 190, Makhfi 191, Bedil 194, Mushtaq 188, Sauda 200, Dard 203, Esrar Dede 205, Hatif 206, Mir 208, Aatish 211, Zauq 213, Dabir 215, Anees 216, Hali 218, Shad 220, Iqbal 222, Khalili 225, Rahi 229, Nurbakhsh, Paul 232. Pages… 244.

RUBAI'YAT OF THE WORLD: An Anthology
Court, Sufi, Dervish, Satirical, Ribald, Prison and Social Poetry in the Ruba'i form from the 9th to the 20th century from the Arabic, Persian, Turkish and Urdu Translations, Introduction and Notes by Paul Smith

Introduction includes chapter on the ruba'i. Included with each selection of a particular poet is a brief biography plus a list of further reading.

THE POETS... Hanzalah page 11, Mansur-al Hallaj 12, Shibli 15, Abu Shakur 16, Shahid 17, Rudaki 18, Rabi'a Balkhi 122, Daqiqi 24, Umarah 27, Firdausi 28, Baba Tahir 31, Farrukhi 36, Asjadi 38, Unsuri 39, Abu Said 42, Ibn Sina 49, Baba Kuhi 52, Azraqi 54, Qatran 56, Ansari 58, Al-Ghazali 61, Mas'ud Sad 63, Mu'izzi 68, Hamadani 71, Omar Khayyam 74, Sana'i 77, Sabir 82, Mahsati 83, Jabali 93, Vatvat 95, Anvari 98, Khaqani 103, Zahir 108, Nizami 111, Ruzbihan 113, Baghdadi 115, 'Attar 118, Auhad ud-din Kermani 126, Kamal ad-din 132, Hamavi 136, Baba Afzal 139, Rumi 142, Imami 153, Hamgar 154, Sadi 158, Iraki 165, Sultan Valad 161, Humam 173, Amir Khusraw 176, Simnani 180, Ibn Yamin 183, Khaju 185, Obeyd Zakani 188, Emad 193, Salman 195, Hafiz 197, Ruh Attar 206, Kadi Burhan-ud-din 208, Jahan Khatun 210, Shah Shuja 220, Kamal 223, Maghribi 224, Bushaq 227, Kasim Anwar 232, Shah Ni'tmu'llah 234, Nesimi 237, Jami 241, Nejati 244, Baba Fighani 246, Babur 248, Humayan 251, Kamran 254, Fuzuli 256, Ghazali 254, Kahi 257, Akbar 258, Urfi 260, Hayati 263, Ulfati 264, Qutub Shah 269, Haleti 271, Dara Shikoh 274, Sarmad 277, Sa'ib 285, Nasir Ali 287, Makhfi 289, Nabi 292, Bedil 294, Nedim 300, Mushtaq 302, Sauda 305. Dard 308, Esrar Dede 311, Nishat 313, Hatif 315, Mir 317, Aatish 321, Zauq 323, Ghalib 325, Momin 329, Dabir 332, Anees 334, Hali 337, Akbar Allahbadi 339, Shad 341, Iqbal 343, Mehroom 347, Firaq 349, Josh 352, Khalili 357, Rahi 361, Faiz, Nurbaksh 364. Pages 367.

LOVE'S AGONY & BLISS: ANTHOLOGY OF URDU POETRY
Sufi, Dervish, Court and Social Poetry from the 16th-20th Century
Translations, Introductions, Etc. by Paul Smith
Introduction includes...The Urdu Language, Urdu Poetry, The Ghazal in Urdu Poetry, Ghazal Singing in India & Pakistan, The Ruba'i in Urdu Poetry, The Masnavi in Urdu Poetry, Glossary for Sufi & Dervish Urdu Poetry. Included with each selection of a particular poet is a brief biography plus a list of further reading.

THE POETS...Qutub Shah page 29, Wali 34, Sauda 43, Dard 51, Nazir 60, Mir 74, Aatish 96, Zauq 107, Ghalib 114, Momin 130, Dabir 138, Anees 142, Hali 146, Akbar Allahabadi 150, Shad 152, Iqbal 160, Asghar 170, Mehroom 175, Josh 177, Jigar 187, Huma 196, Firaq 216, Faiz 228. Pages 230.

BREEZES OF TRUTH
Selected Early & Classical Arabic Sufi Poetry
Translations, Introductions, Etc., by Paul Smith
Introduction includes...Sufis: Their Art and Use of Poetry & The Main

Forms in Arabic Sufi Poetry.

Included with each selection of a particular poet is a brief biography plus a list of further reading.

THE POETS... Hazrat Ali page 19, Ali Ibn Husain 21, Rabi'a of Basra 23, Dhu'l-Nun 36, Bayazid Bistami 47, Al Nuri 50, Junaid 44, Sumnun 65, Mansur al-Hallaj 71, Shibli 101, Ibn Sina 111, Al-Ghazzali 114, Gilani 118, Suhrawadi 122, Ibn al-Farid 129, Ibn 'Arabi 143. Pages 168.

THE~DIVINE~WINE : A Treasury of Sufi and Dervish Poetry (Volume One)
Translations, Introductions, Etc. by Paul Smith
Introduction includes...Sufis & Dervishes: Their Art and Use of Poetry, The Main Forms in Arabic, Persian, Turkish, Kashmiri, Hindi, Urdu, Punjabi, Sindhi & English Sufi & Dervish Poetry.
Glossary of Sufi & Dervish Symbols.
Included with each selection of a particular poet is a brief biography plus a list of further reading.
THE POETS... Hazrat Ali page 39, Ali Ibn Husain 40, Rabi'a of Basra 40, Dhu'l-Nun 46, Bayazid Bistami 53, Al Nuri 54, Junaid 57, Sumnun 59, Mansur al-Hallaj 60, Rudaki 67, Shibli 72, Baba Tahir 74, Abu Said 78, Ibn Sina 85, Baba Kuhi 88, Ansari 90, Al-Ghazzali 92, Hamadani 95, Sana'i 98, Gilani 109, Mahsati 112, Khaqani 117, Suhrawadi 122, Nizami 126, Ruzbihan 150, Baghdadi 152, 'Attar 154, Auhad-ud-din Kermani 177, Kamal ud-din 182, Ibn al-Farid 186, Ibn 'Arabi 197, Baba Farid 206, Hamavi 213, Baba Afzal 216, Rumi 218, Imami 269, Sadi 271, Iraki 341, Sultan Valad 352, Humam 358, Yunus Emre 362, Amir Khusraw 375, Hasan Dihlavi 386, Simnani 388, Auhadi 391, Ibn Yamin 395, Khaju 398, Obeyd Zakani 404, Emad 417, Lalla Ded 426, Hafiz 429, Jahan Khatun 490. Pages 510.

THE - DIVINE - WINE: A Treasury of Sufi and Dervish Poetry (Volume Two)
Translations, Introductions, Etc. by Paul Smith
Introduction includes...Sufis & Dervishes: Their Art and Use of Poetry... The Main Forms in Arabic, Persian, Turkish, Kashmiri, Hindi, Urdu, Punjabi, Pusthu, Sindhi & English Sufi & Dervish Poetry.
Glossary of Sufi Symbols.
Included with each selection of a particular poet is a brief biography plus a list of further reading. THE POETS: Ruh Attar page 39, Haydar 47, Junaid Shirazi 58, Ahmedi 62, Kadi Burhan-ud-din 66, Kamal 70, Maghribi 74, Nesimi 83, Sheykhi 95, Kasim Anwar 97, Shah Ni'matu'llah 104, Kabir 110, Jami 125, Fighani 141, Pir Sultan 147, Khayali 150, Fuzuli 156, Huda'i 167,

TONGUES ON FIRE: An Anthology of the Sufi, Dervish, Warrior & Court Poetry of Afghanistan.
Translations, Introductions, Etc. by Paul Smith
Introduction includes… The Main Forms in Dari/Persian, and Pushtu Poetry; Sufis & Dervishes: Their Art and Use of Poetry. Glossary. Included with each selection of a particular poet is a brief biography plus a list of further reading. THE POETS… Hanzalah page 19, Abu Shakur 21, Shahid 24, Rudaki 27, Rabai'a Balkhi 38, Daqiqi 47, Nasir-i-Khusraw 55, Ansari 59, Azraqi 63, Sana'i 66, Zahir 81, Rumi 96, Imami 151, Jami 155, Mirza 176, Khushal 194, Ashraf Khan 212, Bedil 219, Abdul-Kadir 229, Rahman Baba 237, Khwaja Mohammad 257, Hamid 270, Ahmad Shah 287, Shaida 297, Khalili 303. 307 pages.

THE SEVEN GOLDEN ODES (QASIDAS) OF ARABIA
(The *Mu'allaqat*)
Translations, Introduction & Notes by Paul Smith
The *Mu'allaqat* is the title of a group of seven long Arabic odes or *qasidas* that have come down from the time before Islam. Each is considered the best work of these pre-Islamic poets. The name means 'The Suspended *Qasidas*' or 'The Hanging Poems', the traditional explanation being that these poems were hung on or in the Kaaba at Mecca.
These famous ancient Arabic *qasidas* are formed of three parts: they start, with a nostalgic opening in which the poet reflects on what has passed, known as *nasib*. A common concept is the pursuit of the poet of the caravan of his love; by the time he reaches their campsite they have already moved on. The second section is *rahil* (travel section) in which the poet contemplates the harshness of nature and life away from the tribe. Finally there is the message of the poem, which can take several forms: praise of the tribe, *fakhr*; satire about other tribes, *hija*; or some moral maxims, *hikam*. Included with each qasida of each poet is a brief biography plus a list of

further reading. CONTENTS: The Introduction... The *Mu'allaqat* 7, The *Qasida* 17, The Poets... Imra'ul-Qays 19, Tarafa 37, Amru 59, Harith 73, Antara 83, Zuhair 103, Labid 119. Appendix... Kab's *Qasida* of the Mantle 139. Pages... 144.

THE QASIDA: A WORLD ANTHOLOGY
Translations, Introduction & Notes by Paul Smith

The *qasida* is a form of praise poetry from pre-Islamic Arabia. It sometimes runs to more than 50 lines and sometimes more than 100. It was later inherited by the Persians, the Turks, the Afghans and Urdu Poets where it was developed immensely by Sufi, court and tribal poets. The *qasida* resembles a *ghazal* in many ways except that it is longer. In the first couplet, both the lines rhyme, and the same rhyme runs through the whole poem, the rhyme-word being at the end of the second line of each couplet (after the first couplet).

Included with each selection of a particular poet is a brief biography plus a list of further reading.

IBN AL-FARID: WINE & THE MYSTIC'S PROGRESS
Translation, Introduction & Notes by Paul Smith

Umar Ibn al-Farid, an Egyptian poet (1181-1235), is considered to be the undisputed master of Islamic mystical poetry into Arabic. He is considered not only to be a poet but a Perfect Master *(Qutub)* a God-realised soul... and it is his journey to unity with God that he reveals in probably the longest *qasida* (ode) in Arabic (761 couplets), his famous *Mystic's Progress*. The other poem for which he is most known is his *Wine Poem* that is often seen as a prologue to the *Mystic's Progress*.

Although this long poem has been translated into English 3 times before this is the first time in the correct rhyme of the *qasida* and in clear, concise, modern English.

Included in the Introduction are chapters on his Life & Work, The *Qasida* in Arabic, Previous *Qasidas* that would have influenced him, The Perfect Master *(Qutub)*, and the *Mystic's Progress*. Appendix upon the other 3 translations into English. 200 pages.

HEARTS WITH WINGS Anthology of Persian Sufi and Dervish Poetry
Translations, Introductions, Etc., by Paul Smith
CONTENTS: Introduction…Persian Poetry: A New Beginning… Sufis & Dervishes: Their Art and Use of Poetry… The Main Forms in Persian Sufi & Dervish Poetry… Glossary.

Included with each selection of a particular poet is a brief biography plus a list of further reading. THE POETS… Rudaki 41, Baba Tahir 46, Abu Said 50, Ibn Sina 57, Baba Kuhi 59, Ansari 61, Al-Ghazzali 63, Hamadani 66, Sana'i 69, Mahsati 81, Khaqani 86, Nizami 92, Ruzbihan 117, Baghdadi 119, 'Attar 121, Auhad-ud-din Kermani 144, Kamal ud-din 149, Hamavi 153, Baba Afzal 156, Rumi 159, Imami 210, Sadi 212, Iraki 282, Sultan Valad 284, Humam 286, Amir Khusraw 290, Hasan Dihlavi 302, Simnani 304, Auhadi 307, Ibn Yamin 312, Khaju 315, Obeyd Zakani 324, Emad 334, Hafiz 344, Jahan Khatun 405, Ruh Attar 436, Haydar 444, Junaid Shirazi 356, Kamal 460, Maghribi 464, Kasim Anwar 474, Shah Ni'matu'llah 482, Jami 489, Fighani 506, Urfi 511, Sa'ib 515, Dara Shikoh 518, Sarmad 529, Nasir Ali 531, Makhfi 533, Bedil 567, Mushtaq 575, Hatif 579, Tahirah 586, Iqbal 595, Khalili 603, Nurbaksh 607. Pages 608

RUBA'IYAT OF ABU SA'ID
Translation. Introduction & Notes by Paul Smith.
Abu Sa'id ibn Abi 'l-Khair (968-1049) was a Perfect Master and a poet who lived in Nishapur and composed only *ruba'is,* over 400 of them. He was a founder of Sufi poetry and a major influence on the *ruba'i* and most poets that followed, especially Sana'i, Nizami, 'Attar, Rumi and Hafiz. Here are 188 of his poems translated into the correct form. Included in the Introduction is the life of Abu Sa'id and a history of the *ruba'i* and examples by its greatest exponents. Selected Bibliography. The correct rhyme-structure has been kept as well as the beauty and meaning of these immortal four-line poems. 227 pages.

RUBA'IYAT OF SARMAD
Translation, Introduction & Notes by Paul Smith
Sarmad (d. 1659) or Hazrat Sarmad Shaheed, whose name 'Sarmad' derives from the Persian word for eternal or everlasting, was a famous and infamous Persian dervish poet of Jewish and Armenian origin. As a merchant he gathered his wares and travelled to India to sell them. In India he renounced Judaism and adopted Islam: he later renounced it in favour of Hinduism which he finally renounced for Sufism. He was known for exposing and ridiculing the major religions and hypocrisy of his day, but he also wrote beautiful mystical poetry in the form of 321 *rubai's* (all here translated). He wandered the streets and the courts of the emperor as a naked dervish. He was beheaded in 1659 by Emperor Aurangzeb for his perceived heretical poetry. His grave is located near the Jama Masjid in Delhi. 372 pages.

RUBA'IYAT OF BABA TAHIR
Translations, Introduction & Notes by Paul Smith
Baba Tahir, or Oryan ('The Naked') of Hamadan… approx. 990-1065, was a great God-intoxicated, or God-mad soul *(mast)* and possibly a *Qutub* (Perfect Master) who composed about 120 known *ruba'i* in a simpler metre than the usual *'hazaj'* metre. His simple, mystical poems that he would sing while wandering naked throughout the land had a profound influence on Sufis and dervishes and other *ruba'i* composers, especially Abu Sa'id, Ibn Sina and Omar Khayyam. Included in the Introduction is the life of Baba Tahir and a history of the *ruba'i* and examples by its greatest exponents. Selected Bibliography. The correct rhyme-structure has been kept as well as the beauty and meaning of these immortal four-line poems. 152 pages.

RUBA'IYAT OF JAMI
Translation, Introduction & Notes by Paul Smith
Jami (1414-1493), considered the last great poet of the Classical Period (10th-15thC.) is mostly known for his masterpiece seven *masnavis* epics… including *Joseph and Zulaikh, Layla and Majnun,* and *Salman and Absal.* He also composed three *Divans* consisting of *ghazals rubai's* and other profound mystical poems. Here are 103 *ruba'is,* the largest number ever put into English. Included in the Introduction is the life of Jami and a history of the *ruba'i* and examples by its greatest exponents. Selected Bibliography. The correct rhyme-structure has been kept as well as the beauty and meaning of these beautiful, mystical four-line poems. 177 Pages.

THE POETS OF SHIRAZ
Sufi, Dervish, Court & Satirical Poets from the 9th to the 20th Centuries
of the fabled city of Shiraz
Translations & Introduction & Notes by Paul Smith
CONTENTS: Shiraz in History. The Various Forms in Classical
Persian Poetry, Sufism in Persian Poetry, A Glossary of Sufi & Dervish
Poetry THE POETS OF SHIRAZ... Mansur al-Hallaj 49, Baba Kuhi 57,
Ruzbihan 59, Sadi 63, Nasir 115, Khaju 119, Obeyd 128, Emad 177, Shahin
189, Hafiz 208, Ruh Attar 284, Haydar 298, Azad 311, Junaid 315, Jalal 319,
Jahan 320, Shah Shuja 362, Bushaq 366, Ahli 379, Figani 381, Urfi 386, Visal
391, Qa'ani 392, Shurida 399, Lotfali Suratgar 401. 402 Pages.

RUBA'IYAT OF 'ATTAR
Translation, Introduction & Notes by Paul Smith
Farid ad-din 'Attar (d. 1230) is the Perfect Master Poet who was the author
of over forty books of poetry and prose including *The Conference of the
Birds, The Book of God* (which he is said to have presented to Rumi when
he met him) and *The Lives of the Saints.* Apart from his many books in
masnavi form he also composed many hundreds of mystical *ghazals* and
ruba'is. He also changed the evolution of the *ruba'i* form by composing a
long Sufi epic, the *Mukhtar-nama,* where each of 2088 *ruba'is* is connected
by subject matter that Fitzgerald attempted to do with those he attributed
to Omar Khayyam. Included in the Introduction is the life of 'Attar and a
history of the *ruba'i* and examples by its greatest exponents. Selected
Bibliography. The correct rhyme-structure has been kept as well as the
beauty and meaning of these immortal four-line poems. 111 Pages.

RUBA'IYAT OF MAHSATI
Translation , Introduction & Notes by Paul Smith
We know little of Mahsati Ganjavi's life (1098-1185) except that she lived in
Ganjeh where Sultan Sanjar reigned and as she was a poet at his court she
would have known Anvari. She was a court, dervish and ribald poet. She
knew Nizami (she is said to have been buried in his mausoleum) and Omar
Khayyam... and like Omar composed only in the *ruba'i* form and must be
considered not only a master of that form but also to have helped
revolutionize it. She was an influence on perhaps Iran's greatest female poet
Jahan Khatun of Shiraz and Iran's greatest satirist Obeyd Zakani. She was
famous and also infamous for her liberated behaviour. Included in the
Introduction is the life of Mahsati and a history of the *ruba'i* and examples
by its greatest exponents. Selected Bibliography. The correct rhyme-

structure has been kept as well as the beauty and meaning of these immortal four-line poems. 114 Pages.

RUBA'IYAT OF JAHAN KHATUN
Translation by Paul Smith & Rezvaneh Pashai
Introduction & Notes by Paul Smith
Jahan Khatun (1326-1416?) was the daughter of the king of one of Shiraz's most turbulent times... Masud Shah; pupil and lifelong friend of the world's greatest mystical, lyric poet, Hafiz of Shiraz; the object of crazed desire by (among others) Iran's greatest satirist, the obscene, outrageous, visionary poet Obeyd Zakani; lover, then wife of womanizer Amin al-Din, a minister of one of Persia's most loved, debauched and tragic rulers... Abu Ishak. She was cruelly imprisoned for twenty years under the Muzaffarids while her young daughter mysteriously died; open-minded and scandalous, one of Iran's first feminists... the beautiful and sensuous, petite princess who abdicated her royalty twice is one of Iran's greatest classical lyric poets whose Divan is four times larger than that of Hafiz's and contains about 2000 ghazals and many hundreds of wonderful ruba'is. Included in the Introduction is the life of Jahan and a history of the ruba'i and examples by its greatest exponents. Selected Bibliography. The correct rhyme-structure has been kept as well as the beauty and meaning of these immortal four-line poems. 154 Pages.

RUBA'IYAT OF SANA'I
Translation, Introduction & Notes by Paul Smith
One of the most prolific and influential Sufi Master Poets of all time Hakim Sana'i (d.1131) composed many *ghazals, masnavis* and <u>over 400</u> *ruba'is* that influenced all the *ruba'i* writers that followed him, especially Mahsati and 'Attar. His long *masnavi* (rhyming couplets) mystical work *The Enclosed Garden of the Truth* is said to have had a profound influence on Rumi's composing of his *Masnavi* and in Sadi's composing his *Bustan* ('The Orchard'). Included in the Introduction is the life of Sana'i and a history of the *ruba'i* and examples by its greatest exponents. Selected Bibliography. The correct rhyme-structure has been kept as well as the beauty and meaning of these immortal four-line poems. 109 Pages.

RUBA'IYAT OF HAFIZ
Translation, Introduction & Notes by Paul Smith
Persia's greatest exponent of the *ghazal* Hafiz (1320-1392) became a Perfect Master (*Qutub*), was twice exiled from his beloved Shiraz for his criticism of rulers and false Sufi masters and hypocritical clergy. His *Divan* shows he

composed in other forms including the *ruba'i* of which about 160 survive. As with his *ghazals*, his *ruba'is* are sometimes mystical and sometimes critical of the hypocrisy of his times. Included in the Introduction is the life of Hafiz and a history of the *ruba'i* and examples by its greatest exponents. Selected Bibliography. The correct rhyme-structure has been kept as well as the beauty and meaning of these immortal four-line poems. 220 Pages.

YUNUS EMRE, THE TURKISH DERVISH: SELECTED POEMS
Translation, Introduction & Notes by Paul Smith

Yunus Emre (d. 1320) is considered one of the most important Turkish poets having a great influence on Turkish literature from his own time until today. His poems concern divine love as well as human love of the Divine as God and the Perfect Master, Beloved, Friend and human destiny and weakness. Little is known of his life other than he became a Sufi dervish Perfect Master *(Qutub)*. A contemporary of Rumi, it is told the two great souls met: Rumi asked Yunus what he thought of his huge work, the *Mesnevi*. Yunus said, "Excellent! But I would have done it differently." Surprised, Rumi asked how. Yunus replied, "I'd have written, 'I came from the eternal, clothed myself in flesh, took the name Yunus.'" This illustrates his simple approach that has made him loved by many. His poems were probably a great influence on Hafiz who was born the year he died and who knew Turkish. Here is the largest selection of his poems translated into English mainly in the form of the *gazel* that he often used.

Included… an Introduction on his Life & Times and the Form and History & Function of the *gazel* and a chapter on Sufism & Poetry, Turkish Poetry and the Turkish Language and a Selected Bibliography. Pages… 211

RUBA'IYAT OF KAMAL AD-DIN
Translation, Introduction & Notes by Paul Smith

Kamal ad-din Isma'il (1172-1238) known as 'The Creator of Subtle Thoughts' was the son of the court poet Jamal ad-din and was one of the last of the great poets of the early days in Isfahan. Both father and son praised their city and the same patrons but Kamal ad-din considered himself not only a court poet but a Sufi or Dervish. His *qasidas* in the style of Iraki were greatly admired and some were said to 'reach the summit of perfection' but it is his many much loved human and divine *ruba'is* that his fame now rests upon. Here are the largest number of his *ruba'is* ever put into English. Included in the Introduction… the Life and Times of Kamal ad-din and a history of the *ruba'i* and examples by its greatest exponents and a chapter on Sufi Poetry. The correct rhyme-structure has been kept as well as the beauty and meaning of these beautiful, mystical, loving, sometimes satirical four-line poems. Pages 148.

RUBA'IYAT OF AUHAD UD-DIN
Translation and Introduction by Paul Smith
Auhad ud-din Kermani (1164-1238) was influenced by 'Attar, Ibn 'Arabi (whom he knew) and Suhrawadi and was a powerful speaker and a Sufi Master whose disciples at one time numbered over 70,000.
He used the *ruba'i* form (composing over 1700) in his teaching although he also composed in other forms. Among his followers was Auhadi of Maragha who took his *takhallus* or pen-name from his master. His ideas and behaviour was said to have shocked many of his fellow Sufis and contemporaries. Included in the Introduction… the Life and Work of Auhad ud-din and a history of the *ruba'i* and examples by its greatest exponents and a chapter on Sufi Poetry. The correct rhyme-structure has been kept as well as the beauty and meaning of these mystical, loving four-line poems. 107 pages.

RUBA'YAT OF KHAYYAM
Translation, Introduction & Notes by Paul Smith
Reprint of 1909 Introduction by R.A. Nicholson
Of the 900 to 2000 or so *ruba'is* attributed to Omar Khayyam (died 1132) over 500 years only about ten to twenty percent are now considered to be his. More famous in Iran as an astronomer and mathematician… his nihilistic and hedonistic and occasionally Sufi philosophy in his *ruba'is* meant that his poems were never really popular in his homeland, but of course after the work of FitzGerald the west fell in love with him. Included in the Introduction… the Life and Times of Omar Khayyam and his work as a Scientist & Philosopher and a history of the *ruba'i* and examples by its greatest exponents and a chapter on the various translations into English and other languages. Selected bibliography. The correct rhyme-structure has been kept as well as the beauty and meaning of these beautiful, fatalistic, intoxicated, loving, sometimes mystical and satirical 186 four-line poems. 258 pages.

HUMA: SELECTED POEMS OF MEHER BABA
Translation & Introduction by Paul Smith
Merwan S. Irani (1894-1969), known world-wide as Meher Baba, took Huma (Phoenix) as his *takhallus* or pen-name when he composed enlightened *ghazals* in a mixture of Persian, Urdu and Gujarati in his twenties as a realized disciple of the *Qutub* or Perfect Master Upasni

Maharaj, and also later on. He knew the *ghazals* of Hafiz by heart as did his father, the dervish Sheriar Irani, who had originally walked to Pune in India from Khooramshah in Iran. Merwan went on to reveal himself as *Qutub* and later also declared himself as the *Rasool* or Messiah (Avatar). Contents: The Life of Meher Baba... page 7, The Ghazal, its Form and History 21, Selected Bibliography 27 Ghazals 29, Qit'as (Fragments), 83. 92 Pages.

HAFIZ: SELECTED POEMS
Translation, Introduction & Notes by Paul Smith
Persia's greatest exponent of the *ghazal* Hafiz (1320-1390) became a Perfect Master (*Qutub*), was twice exiled from his beloved Shiraz for his criticism of rulers and false Sufi masters and hypocritical clergy. His *Divan* shows he composed in nearly all forms. As with his *ghazals*, his *masnavis, qasidas, qita's, ruba'is* and other poems are sometimes mystical and sometimes critical of the hypocrisy of his times. Included in the Introduction is the Life and Times and Poetry of Hafiz and a history of the various forms. Selected Bibliography. Glossary of Sufi Symbols. The correct rhyme-structure has been kept as well as the beauty and meaning of these immortal four-line poems. 227 Pages.

'ATTAR: SELECTED POETRY
Translation, Introduction & Notes by Paul Smith
Farid ad-din 'Attar is seen with Sana'i and Rumi (who he met and influenced) as one of the three most important Sufi Poet –Masters of the 13th century. He composed over forty books mainly in the epic *masnavi* form of rhyming couplets, his most famous being *The Book of God* and The *Conference of the Birds*. He also composed many powerful mystical poems in the *ghazal* form and in the *ruba'i* form. Here for the first time is a fine selection of his poems in all three forms in the correct-rhyme structure with the beauty and meaning of his immortal poems. Introduction on his Life & Times and Poetry of 'Attar and an essay by Inayat Khan on Sufi Poetry. Selected Bibliography & Glossary. 167 pages.

SANA'I : SELECTED POEMS
Translation, Introduction & Notes by Paul Smith
One of the most prolific and influential Sufi Master Poets of all time Hakim Sana'i (d.1131) composed many *ghazals, masnavis, qasidas, qita's* and over 400 *ruba'is* that influenced all the *ruba'i* writers that followed him. His long *masnavi* (rhyming couplets) mystical work *The Enclosed Garden of the Truth* is said to have had a profound influence on Rumi's composing

of his *Masnavi* and in Sadi's composing his *Bustan* ('The Orchard').
Included in the Introduction are the Life and Times and Poetry of Sana'i
and a history of the various poetic forms that he wrote in. Selected
Bibliography. The correct rhyme-structure has been kept as well as the
beauty and meaning of these immortal poems. 121 Pages.

THE ROSE GARDEN OF MYSTERY: SHABISTARI
Translation by Paul Smith. Introduction by E.H. Whinfield & Paul Smith
The Rose Garden of Mystery was composed as a 1000 couplet long
masnavi poem in the form of questions and answers on spiritual matters by
Mahmud Shabistari of Tabriz in 1317 at the request of his Spiritual Master.
Since then it has been regarded as one of the finest books on Sufism.
E.G. Browne in his classic work, 'History of Persian Literature' calls this
book "On the whole, one of the best manuals of Sufi theosophy that exists."
Rev. John A. Subhan in his 'Sufism, Its Saints and Shrines' states, "We
know little about the life of the author… But his work is important out of all
comparison with the importance of the author because it is a compendium of
Sufi terminology in the form of question and answer."
The correct rhyme-structure has been kept in this complete, modern
translation, as well as the beauty and meaning of this beautiful, mystical,
poem. Selected Bibliography. Pages 182

RUDAKI: SELECTED POEMS
Translation, Introduction & Notes by Paul Smith
Abu 'Abd Allah Ja'far ibn Muhammad Rudaki (858-941) the 'father of
Persian Poetry' and possibly the *ruba'i*, was born in the village of Rudak
near Samarkand. First a wandering 'dervish' poet/minstrel he later served at
the court of the Samanids of Bokhara. Nasr ibn Ahmad summoned him to
his court and he prospered there amassing great wealth. He had 200 slaves
in his retinue… and 400 camels carried his belongings when he travelled.
In 937 he fell out of favour at court (and was blinded at this time as some
commentators suggest) after the death of the prime-minister who had
supported him. His life ended in abject poverty, forgotten by the world at
that time, perhaps the reason why so much of his vast output of 1,300,000
couplets, only 75 *rubai's, ghazals, qasidas* and *qit'as survive* (most are here
translated, the most published). Rudaki's poetry is about the passage of
time, old age, death, fortune's fickleness, importance of the matters of the
heart, the need to be happy. Although he praised kings, nobles and heroes…
his greatest love was knowledge and experience. The Introduction contains:
Persian Poetry, A New Beginning; The Life, Times and Poetry of Rudaki;
The Various Forms in the Poetry of Rudaki and a Selected Bibliography.

The correct rhyme-structure has been kept in this modern translation, as well as the beauty and meaning of these beautiful poems. 128 pages.

SADI: SELECTED POEMS
Translation, Introduction & Notes by Paul Smith
Sadi of Shiraz, along with Hafiz, Nizami & Rumi is considered one of the great mystical and romantic poets of Iran. His masterpieces, *The Rose Garden* and *The Bustan* (Orchard) have been a major influence in the East and West for the past 700 years. His *Divan* of *ghazals* are still much loved by Iranians. His *ruba'is* have also been an influence on the poets that followed him. Here is a large selection of his *ghazals, ruba'is* and *masnavis.* Included is a long Introduction on his Life and Times and Poetry. There is also a Selected Bibliography and Glossary of Sufi Symbols. The correct rhyme-structure has been kept in this modern translation, as well as the beauty and meaning of these beautiful poems. 207 pages.

JAMI: SELECTED POEMS
Translation, Introduction by Paul Smith
Jami (1414-1493), is still considered the last great poet of the Classical Period (10th-15th C.) of Persian Poetry is mostly known for his masterpiece seven *masnavi* epics… including his masterpieces Joseph and Zulaikh… also Layla and Majnun, Chain of Gold and Book of the Wisdom of Alexander. He also composed three *Divans* consisting of *ghazals rubai's* and other profound, mystical poems. Here is the largest number of his *ghazals* and *ruba'is* translated into English and a good selection from most of his *masnavis.* Included in the Introduction… the life of Jami and a chapter of Sufism in Persian Poetry and a chapter on the various forms of poetry he used and a Selected Bibliography. The correct rhyme-structure has been kept as well as the beauty and meaning of these beautiful, mystical poems. 164 Pages.

NIZAMI: SELECTED POEMS
Translation & Introduction by Paul Smith
Nizami (d. 1208) is a true Sufi Master Poet who is most famous for his six books in *masnavi* form: *The Treasury of the Mysteries, Layla and Majnun, Khrosrau and Shirin, The Seven Portraits* and his two books on Alexander. He also composed a *Divan* of approximately 20,000 couplets mostly in *ghazals* and *ruba'is*… tragically only 200 couplets survive. His influence on Attar, Rumi, Sadi, Hafiz and Jami and all others that followed was profound. Here is the largest number of his *ghazals* and *ruba'is* and *qasidas* translated into English and a good selection from his *masnavis.*

Included in the Introduction… the life and Times and Poetry of Nizami and
on the various forms of poetry he used and a Selected Bibliography.
The correct rhyme-structure has been kept as well as the beauty and
meaning of these beautiful, mystical poems. 235 pages.

RUBA'IYAT OF BEDIL
Translation & Introduction by Paul Smith

Mirza Abdul-Qader Bedil (1644-1721) is one of the most respected poets
originally from Afghanistan. In the early 17th century, his family moved
from Balkh to India, to live under the Mughul dynasty. He was born and
educated near Patna. In his later life he spent time travelling and visiting
ancestral lands. His writings in Persian are extensive, being one of the
creators of the 'Indian style'. He had complicated views on the nature of
God, heavily influenced by the Sufis. Bedil's 16 books of poetry contain
nearly 147,000 couplets with over 3600 poems that are *ruba'is*. He is now
considered a great later master of this form. The correct rhyme-structure has
been kept as well as the beauty and meaning of these beautiful and often
mystical poems. 134 pages.

BEDIL: SELECTED POEMS
Translation & Introduction by Paul Smith

Mirza Abdul-Qader Bedil (1644-1721) is one of the most respected poets
from Afghanistan. In the early 17th century, his family moved from Balkh to
India, to live under the Mughul dynasty. He was born and educated near
Patna. In his later life he spent time travelling and visiting ancestral lands.
His writings in Persian are extensive, being one of the creators of the
'Indian style'. Bedil's 16 books of poetry contain nearly 147,000 couplets.
With Ghalib he is considered a master of the complicated 'Indian Style' of
the *ghazal*. He had complicated views on the nature of God, heavily
influenced by the Sufis. The correct rhyme-structure has been kept as well
as the beauty and meaning of these beautiful and often mystical poems.
Pages… 144

ANVARI: SELECTED POEMS
Translation & Introduction by Paul Smith

Ahad-ud-din Anvari Abeverdi (1126-1189) was a court poet of the Seljuk
sultans. Jami composed a *ruba'i* where he names him, along with Firdausi
and Sadi as one of the 'three apostles' of Persian poetry. He was also a
celebrated astronomer, mathematician and scientist who admitted he gave
them up for the more lucrative occupation of … a court poet, that he later
rejected twenty years before his death for a life of seclusion and

contemplation. He is renowned for his delightful wittiness that can be found in many of his *ruba'is* and *qit'as and ghazals*. He is one of the greatest Persian masters of the *qasida* and his one that has been called 'The Tears of Khurasan' is considered his masterpieces. He is known for his sense of humour and sometimes obscenity. He created a new kind of poetry by using the conversational language of his time in simple words and expressions. The correct rhyme-structure has been kept as well as the beauty and meaning of these beautiful, poems. 156 pages.

RUBA'IYAT OF 'IRAQI
Translation & Introduction by Paul Smith
'Iraqi (1213-1289) was the author of a *Divan* of spiritual *ghazals* and *ruba'is* and the famous work in prose and poetry… *Lama'at,* 'Divine Flashes'… a classic of Sufi Mysticism. He was born in Hamadan in western Persia and as a child learnt the *Koran* by heart. He travelled from Persia to India with dervishes where he stayed for 25 years. It is said that on his travels he met Rumi. His grave is in Damascus beside that of another great Perfect Master and poet Ibn al-'Arabi. When seeing these graves a pilgrim stated, "That ('Iraqi) is the Persian Gulf and this (Ibn al-'Arabi) is the Arabian Sea." The correct rhyme-structure has been kept as well as the beauty and meaning of these beautiful, mystical poems. 116 pages.

THE WISDOM OF IBN YAMIN: SELECTED POEMS
Translation & Introduction Paul Smith
Amir Fakhr al-Din Mahmud, or Ibn Yamin (1286-1367), was born in Turkistan. His father was a successful poet who taught him the craft and left his son wealthy and the role of the court-poet in Khurasan. Ibn Yamin was taken captive when war broke out in 1342 and his complete *Divan* of poems was destroyed. He was a master of the form of the *qi'ta*. He is now as he was then, famous for his down-to-earth wisdom. Hafiz was probably influenced by his poems. During the last 25 years of his life he composed a further 5000 couplets on top of those he remembered. Here is the largest translation of his poems published in correct-rhyming, meaningful English. Introduction includes: Life & Times & Poetry, Forms in which he wrote, Bibliography. 155 pages.

RAHMAN BABA: SELECTED POEMS
Translation & Introduction by Paul Smith
Rahman Baba (1652 to 1711) is considered the greatest Sufi Pashtun poet to compose poems, mainly *ghazals*, in the Pushtu language. Born in Mohmand region of Afghanistan near Peshawar he was called 'The Nightingale of

Peshawar'. This was a time of struggle and hardship and in the midst of the turmoil he was an excellent student with a natural gift for poetry.
He eventually questioned the value of such pursuits and withdrew from the world, dedicating himself to prayer and devotion. In solitary worship he began to write again and his poetry spread. Religious figures used it to inspire the devout, political leaders to inspire the independence movement. His *Divan* is 343 poems… *ghazals* and a few *qasidas* and *mukhammas*. Introduction is on his Life & Times & Poetry and the Forms in which he wrote and on Sufism & Poetry. The correct rhyme-structure is kept as well as the meaning of these beautiful, enlightened poems. 141 pages

RUBA'IYAT OF DARA SHIKOH
Translation & Introduction by Paul Smith
Dara Shikoh (1615-1659) was the oldest son of Emperor Shah Jahan and was known to be a loving husband , a good son and loving father. He was a fine poet, his poems having the influence of Sufism to which he was dedicated. He used 'Qadiri' as his *takhallus* or pen-name. His *Divan* of *ghazals, ruba'is* and *qasidas* in Persian was not the only work he left behind, his five prose works on Sufism and mysticism are popular in India even today. His *Majma al-Bahrain* or *The Mingling of the Two Oceans* is an explanation of the mystical sameness of Sufism and Vedanta. He also translated the *Upanishads, Bhagavad Gita and Yoga-Vasishta* into Persian. After he was defeated after leading an uprising against his cruel, fundamentalist brother Emperor Aurangzeb and was brutally killed in 1659. The correct rhyme-structure has been kept and the meaning of these beautiful, mystical poems. This is the largest translation of his poems into English. 120 pages

ANTHOLOGY OF POETRY OF THE CHISTI SUFI ORDER
Translations & Introduction by Paul Smith
The Chishti Order is a Sufi order within the mystic branches of Islam which was founded in Chisht, a small town near Herat, Afghanistan about 930 A.D. The Chishti Order is known for its emphasis on love, tolerance, and openness. The Master & Perfect Master Poets: Mu'in ud-din Chishti, Baba Farid, Nizam –ud-din Auliya, Amir Khusrau, Dara Shikoh, Inayat Khan, Khadim & others. Introduction on the Chishti Order of Sufism and the Spiritual forms of the Master Poets of this famous Order of the Indian Sub-Continent. The correct rhyme-structures have been kept and the meaning of these often beautiful, powerful and always spiritual poems. Pages 300.

POEMS OF MAJNUN
Translation & Introduction by Paul Smith

Qays was a youth, a Bedouin poet in the seventh century of the Bani Amir tribe in the Najd desert. He fell in love with Layla from the same tribe whom he was denied. (It is said that Shakespeare got his Romeo & Juliet from their tragic love story). Most of his recorded poetry was composed before his descent into madness (*mast*) then through a Perfect Master... his spiritual unification with his beloved. Nizami's famous telling of their tale came from this collected poems (*Divan*) and other sources. Hundreds of other Persian, Turkish and Urdu poets imitated him or wrote their own versions of the story of the height of human love that became Divine. Here in the form of the *qit'a* in which they were composed, is the largest collection of poems put into English. 200 pages.

SHAH NI'TMAT'ULLAH VALI: SELECTED POEMS
Translation & Introduction by Paul Smith

Shah Ni'matu'llah Vali (1330-1431) was the founder of an order of Sufis that is today the largest in Iran. As well as a Sufi Master he was a poet who at times used 'Sayyid' as his *takhallus* or pen-name. He was influenced Ibn 'Arabi and Hafiz. He came from Aleppo or Shiraz and after studies travelled in Egypt, Morocco, Mecca (where he met his Spiritual Master Abdullah Yafi'i). He built a monastery in Mahan near Kirman and lived there until his death. He composed many prose works on Sufism and his *Divan* contains over 13,000 couplets, mostly *ghazals* and *ruba'is*. This is the largest selection of his poems published in English. Introduction is on his Life & Times & Poetry and the Forms in which he wrote and on Sufism & Poetry. The correct rhyme-structure has been kept as well as the meaning of these beautiful, enlightened poems. Glossary, bibliography. 148 pages

AMIR KHUSRAU: SELECTED POEMS
Translation & Introduction by Paul Smith

Amir Khusrau (1253-1324), the 'Parrot of India' was born at Patigali near the Ganges in India. At the age of thirty-six he was poet-laureate, serving many sultans. He was not only fluent in Persian, in which he composed the majority of his 92 books, but also in Arabic, Hindi and Sanskrit. He composed ten long *masnavis*, five *Divans* of *ghazals* and other poems and many prose works. He was a Master musician and invented the *sitar*. The Perfect Master Nizam ud-din took him as his disciple and eventually he became God-realized. He rebelled against narrow spirituality and helped redefine the true Sufi way. He was a profound influence on Hafiz and is seen as the link between Sadi and Hafiz in updating the form and content of the *ghazal* and eroticising it. This is the largest selection of his poems in English. Introduction is on his Life & Times & Poetry and the Forms in which he wrote and on Sufism & Poetry. The correct rhyme-structure has been kept and the meaning of these beautiful, enlightened poems. 201 pages

A WEALTH OF POETS: Persian Poetry at the Courts of Sultan Mahmud in Ghazneh & Sultan Sanjar in Ganjeh (998-1158)
Translations, Introduction and Notes by Paul Smith
CONTENTS: Persian Poetry: A New Beginning… 7, Sultan Mahmud: His Life, Times and Poets 9. Sultan Sanjar: His Life, Times & Poets… 17. The Various Forms in Persian Poetry… 22, Sufism in Persian Poetry… 31.
THE POETS: Poets at the Court of Sultan Mahmud… page 35,
Sultan Mahmud 37, Umarah 39, Kisa'i 41, Firdausi 44, Farrukhi 55, Asjadi 67, Manuchirhri 69, Poet-laureate Unsuri 75, Asadi 82.
Poets at the Court of Sultan Sanjar… page 89, Poet-laureate Mu'izzi 91, Sabir 101, Mahsati 105, Jabali 116, Vatvat 120, Anvari 124.
The correct rhyme-structures have been kept and the meaning of these often beautiful, challenging, powerful and sometimes mystical poems. 158 pages

SHIMMERING JEWELS: Anthology of Poetry Under the Reigns of the Mughal Emperors of India (1526-1857)
Translations, Introductions, Etc. by Paul Smith
CONTENTS: The Mughal Empire… Page 7, Emperor Babur… 14, Emperor Humayun… 19, Emperor Akbar… 31, Emperor Jahangir… 44, Emperor Shah Jahan… 50, Emperor Aurangzeb… 57, Emperor Bahadur Shah Zafar… 71. Sufis & Dervishes: Their Art and Use of Poetry… 78, The Main Forms in Persian, Urdu & Pushtu Poetry of the Indian Sub-Continent… 81. Poets in the Reign of Babur… 91, Babur 93, Wafa'i 96, Farighi 97, Haqiri 98. Poets in the Reign of Humayun… 99, Humayun 102, Kamran 104, Nadiri 106, Bayram 107. Poets in the Reign of Akbar… 109, Akbar 111, Ghazali 113, Maili 116, Kahi 117, Faizi 119, Urfi 122, Nami 127, Hayati 130, Qutub Shah 132, Naziri 135. Poets in the Reign of Jahangir… 137, Jahangir 139, Rahim 140, Talib 142, Shikebi 160, Tausani 161, Qasim 162. Poets in the Reign of Shah Jahan… 163, Qudsi 165, Sa'ib 168, Kalim 172. Poets in Reign of Aurangzeb… 177, Dara Shikoh 179, Mullah Shah 186, Sarmad 189, Khushal 199, Nasir Ali 213, Makhfi 215, Wali 239, Bedil 243. Poets in the Reign of Bahadur Shah Zafar… 251, Zafar 253, Zauq 260, Ghalib 266, Momin 275, Shefta 280, Dagh 283. The correct rhyme-structures have been kept and the meaning of these often beautiful, powerful and sometimes mystical poems. Pages 292.

RAHMAN BABA: SELECTED POEMS
Translation & Introduction by Paul Smith

Rahman Baba (1652 to 1711) is considered the greatest Sufi Pashtun poet to compose poems, mainly *ghazals,* in the Pushtu language. Born in Mohmand region of Afghanistan near Peshawar he was called 'The Nightingale of Peshawar'. This was a time of struggle and hardship and in the midst of the turmoil he was an excellent student with a natural gift for poetry.
He eventually questioned the value of such pursuits and withdrew from the world, dedicating himself to prayer and devotion. In solitary worship he began to write again and his poetry spread. Religious figures used it to inspire the devout, political leaders to inspire the independence movement. His *Divan* is 343 poems… *ghazals* and a few *qasidas* and *mukhammas.* Introduction is on his Life & Times & Poetry and the Forms in which he wrote and on Sufism & Poetry. The correct rhyme-structure is kept as well as the meaning of these beautiful, enlightened poems. 139 pages

RUBA'IYAT OF DARA SHIKOH
Translation & Introduction by Paul Smith

Dara Shikoh (1615-1659) was the oldest son of Emperor Shah Jahan and was known to be a loving husband , a good son and loving father. He was a fine poet, his poems having the influence of Sufism to which he was dedicated. He used 'Qadiri' as his *takhallus* or pen-name. His *Divan* of *ghazals, ruba'is* and *qasidas* in Persian was not the only work he left behind, his five prose works on Sufism and mysticism are popular in India even today. His *Majma al-Bahrain* or *The Mingling of the Two Oceans* is an explanation of the mystical sameness of Sufism and Vedanta. He also translated the *Upanishads, Bhagavad Gita and Yoga-Vasishta* into Persian. After he was defeated after leading an uprising against his cruel, fundamentalist brother Emperor Aurangzeb and was brutally killed in 1659. The correct rhyme-structure has been kept and the meaning of these beautiful, powerful mystical poems. This is the largest translation of his poems into English. 120 pages

ANTHOLOGY OF POETRY OF THE CHISHTI SUFI ORDER
Translations & Introduction by Paul Smith

The Chishti Order is a Sufi order within the mystic branches of Islam which was founded in Chisht, a small town near Herat, Afghanistan about 930 A.D. The Chishti Order is known for its emphasis on love, tolerance, and openness. The Master & Perfect Master Poets: Mu'in ud-din Chishti, Baba Farid, Nizam –ud-din Auliya, Amir Khusrau, Dara Shikoh, Inayat

Khan, Khadim & others. Introduction on the Chishti Order of Sufism and the Spiritual forms of the Master Poets of this famous Order of the Indian Sub-Continent. The correct rhyme-structures have been kept and the meaning of these often beautiful, powerful and always spiritual poems. Pages 300.

POEMS OF MAJNUN
Translation & Introduction by Paul Smith
Qays was a youth, a Bedouin poet in the seventh century of the Bani Amir tribe in the Najd desert. He fell in love with Layla from the same tribe whom he was denied. (It is said that Shakespeare got his Romeo & Juliet from their tragic love story). Most of his recorded poetry was composed before his descent into madness *(mast)* then through a Perfect Master... his spiritual unification with his beloved. Nizami's famous telling of their tale came from this collected poems *(Divan)* and other sources. Hundreds of other Persian, Turkish and Urdu poets imitated him or wrote their own versions of the story of the height of human love that became Divine. Here in the form of the *qit'a* in which they were composed, is the largest collection of poems put into English. Included are four Appendixes. 220 pages.

RUBA'IYAT OF ANSARI
Translation & Introduction by Paul Smith
One of the greatest mystical poets and Perfect Masters of all time, Abdullah Ansari... who passed from this world 1089 in Herat was most famous for his biographical dictionary on saints and Sufi masters and his much loved collection of inspiring prayers, the *Munajat* among many works in Persian and Arabic. His *ruba'is* appear throughout his works. The correct rhyme-structure has been kept and the meaning of these beautiful, powerful, mystical poems. This is the largest translation of his *ruba'is* into English. 183 pages

RUBA'IYAT OF SHAH NI'TMATULLAH VALI
Translation & Introduction by Paul Smith
Shah Ni'matullah Vali (1330-1431) was the founder of an order of Sufis that is today the largest in Iran. As well as a Sufi Master he was a poet who at times used 'Sayyid' as his *takhallus* or pen-name. He was influenced by Ibn 'Arabi and Hafiz. He came from Aleppo and after studies travelled in Egypt, Morocco, Mecca (where he met his Spiritual Master Abdullah Yafi'i). He built a monastery in Mahan near Kirman and lived there until his death. He composed many prose works on Sufism and his *Divan*

contains over 13,000 couplets, mostly *ghazals* and *ruba'is*. This is the largest selection of his *ruba'is* published in English. Introduction is on his Life & Times & Poetry and the meaning of Sufi poetry and a History of the Form and Function of the *Ruba'i*. The correct rhyme-structure has been kept as well as the meaning of these beautiful, enlightened poems. Glossary, bibliography. 125 pages

ANSARI: SELECTED POEMS
Translation & Introduction by Paul Smith
One of the greatest mystical poets and Perfect Masters of all time, Abdullah Ansari... who passed from this world 1089 in Herat was most famous for his biographical dictionary on saints and Sufi masters and his much loved collection of inspiring prayers, the *Munajat* among many works in Persian and Arabic. His *ruba'is* appear throughout his works and he composed three *Divans* in which his *ghazals* are in the majority. Here is a fine selection of them and a *qasida*. The correct rhyme-structure has been kept and the meaning of these beautiful, powerful, mystical poems. This is the largest translation of his poems into English. 156 pages

BABA FARID: SELECTED POEMS
Translation & Introduction by Paul Smith
The father of Punjabi poetry Baba Farid (1173-1266) was born in the Punjab. Khwaja Bakhtiar Kaki was Baba Farid's Spiritual Master. Kaki met Mu'in ud-din Chishti at Baghdad and became his disciple. The king at Delhi, Balban, welcomed Farid in Delhi. His daughter married Farid. Baba Farid, the Sufi Master poet laureate from Punjab is famous for his wise and spiritual couplets *(slokas)*... 112 of them are in the bible of the Sikhs (whom he influenced) the *Guru Granth,* and 128 are translated here with the correct rhyme-structure and meaning. Hospitals and factories and even a town named after him. 164 pages.

POETS OF THE NI'MATULLAH SUFI ORDER
Translations & Introduction by Paul Smith
Shah Ni'matullah (1330-1431) was the founder of an order of Sufis that is today one of the largest in Iran and around the world. As well as a Sufi Master he was a poet who inspired many Spiritual Masters and Sufi Poets over the following 500 years to follow his example.
CONTENTS: The Ni'matullah Sufi Order... page 7, Sufis & Dervishes: Their Art & Use of Poetry... 10, Forms of Poetry used by the Ni'matullah Poets... 26, Selected Bibliography... 35, Glossary... 36

The Poets...Shah Ni'matullah... 39, Bushaq... 85, Kasim Anwar... 117, Shah Da'i... 145, Nur 'Ali Shah... 167, Bibi Hayati... 178, Rida 'Ali Shah... 209, Muzaffar 'Ali Shah... 221, Khusrawi... 230, Munis 'Ali Shah... 236. The correct rhyme-structures have been kept and the meaning of these beautiful, powerful and mystical poems. This is the largest translation of their poems into English. 244 pages.

MU'IN UD-DIN CHISHTI: SELECTED POEMS
Translation & Introduction by Paul Smith
Mu'in ud-din Chishti (1141-1230) was also known as *Gharib Nawaz* or 'Benefactor of the Poor', he is the most famous Sufi saint of the Chishti Order of the Indian Subcontinent. He also composed many *ghazals* . In his book *Pre Mughal Persian in Hindustan,* Muhammad 'Abdu'l Ghani states... "He was the greatest lyric poet of his age. His style is exuberant and precise at once. His poems are a storehouse of transcendental thoughts beautifully ordered and forcefully expressed. There is always a sense of pious serenity and joy in his verses which are teeming with Divine Love... his poetry resembles closely that of Hafiz... He takes his readers along with him solely to spiritual ecstasy and gives them a peep into the ethereal world..." Today, hundreds of thousands of people... Muslims, Hindus, Christians and others take grace from his tomb and poems. This is the largest selection of his *ghazals* translated into English in the correct form and meaning. 171 pages.

QASIDAH BURDAH:
THE THREE POEMS OF THE PROPHET'S MANTLE
Translations & Introduction by Paul Smith
Ka'b ibn Zuhair (died 7th century A.D.) was a famous poet who at first opposed Prophet Muhammad. Finally, he secretly went to Medina and approached the Prophet to ask if one who repented and embraced the faith would be forgiven. Mohammed answered yes and the poet asked, "Even Ka'b ibn Zuhair?" When he affirmed this, Ka'b revealed his identity and read a poem, his *Banat Suad* (of 55 couplets), which would become his most famous poem. As a reward Prophet Mohammed took off his mantle (cloak) and put it on Ka'b's shoulders. The second 'Mantle' qasida (ode) of praise for Mohammed was composed by the eminent Sufi, Imam al-Busiri (1210-1297). The poem (161 couplets) is famous mainly in the Sunni Muslim world. It is entirely in praise of Prophet Mohammed, who is said to have cured the poet of paralysis by appearing to him in a dream and wrapping him in a mantle. The third poet of the 'Mantle' was Ahmed Shawqi (1869 - 1932) the great Arabic Poet-Laureate, an Egyptian poet and dramatist who pioneered

the modern Egyptian literary movement, most notably introducing the genre of poetic epics to the Arabic literary tradition. His 'Mantle' *qasida* is 190 couplets. The correct rhyme-structure has been kept and the meaning of these beautiful, powerful, spiritual poems. Pages 116

KHUSHAL KHAN KHATTAK: THE GREAT POET & WARRIOR OF AFGHANISTAN, SELECTED POEMS
Translation & Introduction by Paul Smith
Khushal Khan Khattak (1613-1689) was a Pashtun poet, warrior, and chief of the Khattak tribe. He wrote in Pashtu during the reign of the Mughals and fought the fanatic Aurangzeb and admonished Afghans to forsake their divisive tendencies and unite. He was the father of fifty-seven sons, some of them fine poets and thirty daughters. He is the author of over 200 works in Pushtu and Persian, consisting of Poetry, Medicine, Ethics, Religious Jurisprudence, Philosophy, Falconry, etc., together with an account of the events of his own life. His poetry is said to consist of more than 45,000 poems! There is not another poet in the Afghan language of Pashtu who created so many poems on such a wide range of subjects. He wrote *ghazals, ruba'is, qasidas, qi'tas* and *masnavis.* Introduction on his life, times & poetry. The correct rhyme-structure has been kept and the meaning of these beautiful, powerful, and occasionally spiritual poems. Pages 187

'IRAQI: SELECTED POEMS
Translation & Introduction by Paul Smith
'Iraqi (1213-1289) was the author of a *Divan* of spiritual *ghazals* and *ruba'is* and the famous work in prose and poetry... *Lama'at,* 'Divine Flashes'... a classic of Sufi Mysticism. He was born in Hamadan in western Persia and as a child learnt the *Koran* by heart. He travelled from Persia to India with dervishes where he stayed for 25 years. It is said that on his travels he met Rumi. His grave is in Damascus beside that of another great Perfect Master and poet Ibn al-'Arabi. When seeing these graves a pilgrim stated, "That ('Iraqi) is the Persian Gulf and this (Ibn al-'Arabi) is the Arabian Sea." Introduction: The Life & Times & Poems of 'Iraqi, Selected Bibliography, Forms in Classical Persian Poetry Used by 'Iraqi. *Rubai's, Ghazals, Qasida, Masnavis, Tarji-band.* The correct rhyme-structure has been kept as well as the beauty and meaning of these beautiful, mystical poems. 158 pages.

RUBA'IYAT OF BABA AFZAL
Translation & Introduction by Paul Smith

Baba Afzal (1186-1256) came from Maraq near Kashan. He is the author of many Persian works on philosophical and metaphysical subjects and translated the Arabic version of Aristotle's 'The Book of the Soul' into Persian. He was a Sufi and the author of about 500 mystical and at times controversial *ruba'is* some that have been mistakenly identified as Khayyam's. Some of the themes in these include warnings about the futility of involvement with the things of the world, correspondence between microcosm and macrocosm and self-knowledge as the goal of human existence. He is one of the greatest poets among the philosophers of Islam. Introduction includes: The Life, Times & Work of Baba Afzal, Sufis: Their Art & Use of Poetry, The *Ruba'i:* Its Form, Use & History. The correct rhyme-structure has been kept as well as the beauty and meaning of these poems. 178 pages.

RIBALD POEMS OF THE SUFI POETS
Sana'i, Anvari, Mahsati, Rumi, Sadi, Obeyd Zakani
Translations, Introductions Paul Smith

Some of the greatest of the Persian Sufi poets composed ribald and at times 'obscene' poems for satirical and often (as in the case of Rumi) for teaching some spiritual truth or moral. Here is a wide-ranging selection of the greatest of them from the eleventh to the fourteenth century. Here are at times hilarious, witty, weird, and erotic and obscene poems in most of the various forms of classical Persian poetry… the *ghazal,* the *ruba'i,* the *masnavi,* the *qit'a,* the *qasida* and the *tarji-band.* 190 pages.

RUMI: SELECTIONS FROM HIS *MASNAVI*
Translation & Introduction by Paul Smith

The *masnavi* is the form used in Persian and other languages to write epic ballads or romances and it is essentially a Persian invention. The most famous poems written in this form are the 'Shahnama' (Book of the Kings) of Firdausi, the 'Enclosed Garden of the Truth' of Sana'i, the 'Five Treasures' of Nizami, the 'Conference of the Birds' and 'The Book of God' and many others by 'Attar, the 'Seven Thrones' of Jami, the ten *masnavis* of Amir Khusrau and of course the greatest of them all… the *'Masnavi'* of Rumi. Many *masnavis* by the great Perfect Master Poets were of a Sufi/Dervish mystical nature. Included in this volume is a chapter on The Life, Times & Poetry of Rumi and one on the history of the *masnavi* in Persian poetry by the various masters in this form with translations of their works up until Rumi. From Rumi's *Masnavi* are his Introduction to the 6 volumes and the first three Tales in full and excerpts from the whole work, including some of his ribald tales. Selected Bibliography. The correct rhyme-form of the *masnavi* has been kept in all the translations. 260 pages.

WINE OF LOVE: AN ANTHOLOGY,
Wine in the Poetry of Arabia, Persia, Turkey & the Indian Sub-Continent
from Pre-Islamic Times to the Present
Translations & Introduction by Paul Smith
CONTENTS Arabic Poetry 7, Persian Poetry 11, Turkish Poetry 13, Pushtu Poetry 15, Urdu Poetry 17, The Main Forms in Arabic, Persian, Turkish, Pushtu & Urdu Poetry 19, Wine in Sufi Poetry 29, Arabic Poetry… 37, Ima'-ul-Qays 39, Antara 47, Tarafa 59, Amru 72, Labid 80, Ka'b 92, Omar Ibn abi Rabi'a 96, Majnun 98, Rabi'a of Basra 101, Abu Nuwas 106, Bayazid Bastami 114, Al-Mutanabbi 116, Al-Ma'arri 131, Gilani 134, Suhrawadi 137, Ibn al-Farid 140, Ibn 'Arabi 145, Al-Shushtari 148. Persian Poetry… 151, Abu Shakur 153, Junaidi 155, Rudaki 157, Agachi 172, Rabi'a Balkhi 174, Daqiqi 177, Umarah 181, Kisa'i 183, Farrukhi 185, Asjadi 193, Minuchihri 195, Unsuri 198, Abu Sa'id 201, Baba Kuhi 203, Qatran 205, Ansari 207, Al-Ghazali 212, Mas'ud Sa'd 214, Mu'izzi 216, Omar Khayyam 219, Sana'I 227, Sabir 232, Mahsati 235, Jabali 238, Vatvat 240, Anvari 242, Falaki 246, Hasan Ghaznavi 249, Athir 252, Mujir 255, Khaqani 257, Mu'in 266, Zahir 274, Nizami 278, Ruzbihan 284, 'Attar 286, Auhad ud-din Kermani 292, Kamal ad-din 294, Baba Afzal 297, Rumi 299, Sadi 310, 'Iraqi 323, Humam 335, Amir Khusray 337, Hasan Dihlavi 347, Khaju 351, Obeyd Zakani 353, Emad 361, Salman 366, Shahin 371, Hafiz 374, Ruh Attar 396, Haydar 401, Junaid Shirazi 404, Jahan Khatun 406, Maghribi 413, Bushaq 415, Kasim Anwar 419, Shah Ni'matu'llah 422, Jami 425, Ahli 428, Helali 430, Fighani 432, Babur 435, Ghazali 437, Urfi 439, Lotfali Suratgar 493, Rahi 495. Turkish Poetry… 497, Ahmed Yesevi 499, Yunus Emre 502, Kadi Burhan-ud-din 507, Nesimi 509, Mihri 515, Necati 518, Pir Sultan 523, Khayali 535, Fuzuli 528, Baqi 535, Huda'I 539, Nef'I 541, Yahya 544, Na'ila 546, Nabi 548, Nedim 550, Fitnet 553, Galib 555, Leyla Khanim 562. Pushtu Poetry… 565, Mirza 567, Khushal 570, Ashraf Khan 578, Abdul-Khadir 580, Rahman Baba 585, Khwaja Mohammad 588, Shaida 592. Urdu Poetry… 595, Wali 587, Sauda 599, Dard 601, Nazir 603, Mir 606, Zauq 610, Ghalib 612, Momin 619, Dagh 621, Shad 623, Iqbal 625, Ashgar 629, Josh 631, Jigar 633, Huma 637, Firaq 641, Faiz 643. 645 pages.

GHALIB: SELECTED POEMS
Translation & Introduction by Paul Smith
Mirza Asadullah Beg (1797-1869), known as Ghalib (conqueror), was born in
the city of Agra of parents with Turkish aristocratic ancestry. When he was
only five his father Abdullah Beg Khan died in a battle while working under
Rao Raja Bakhtwar. Ghalib's fame came to him posthumously. He had
himself remarked during his lifetime that although his age had ignored his
greatness, it would be recognised by later generations. History has
vindicated his claim. Ghalib wrote beautiful *ghazals* and other poems in
Persian… over 250 (many are translated here) but is more famous for his
ghazals written in Urdu. Before Ghalib, the Urdu *ghazal* was primarily an
expression of anguished love, but Ghalib expressed his philosophy and
cynicism on God and other subjects. His Urdu *Divan* contains 263 *ghazals*
and a small number of *ruba'is, masnavis, qasidas* and *qit'as*. There have
been many movies based on his life made in India and Pakistan where his
popularity has never flagged. Introduction on his Life, Poetry and Times
and the Forms of Poetry he wrote in. The correct rhyme-structure has been
kept as well as the beauty and meaning of these poems. Pages 200.

THE ENLIGHTENED SAYINGS OF HAZRAT 'ALI
The Right Hand of the Poet
Translation & Introduction by Paul Smith
Hazrat 'Ali (598-661) was Prophet Mohammed's nephew, son-in-law and
favourite and was the first Imam of the Shi'ites and the fourth of the true
caliphs of the Sunnis. Sufi Masters believe in Ali as one of the 'Seven
Great Ones' in the first generation of teachers and many in orders of
Dervishes trace their spiritual ancestry back to him. Hazrat Ali's sayings
are published as *Nahj al-Balagh* or 'The Peak of Experience'… a treasury of
wisdom and divine grace. It is said that he wrote the original *Koran* in his
own blood as Prophet Mohammed gave it. He also composed a *Divan* of
enlightened poetry and one of his important, profound *ghazals* is translated
in the Introduction to this book. Pages 260.

HAFIZ: TONGUE OF THE HIDDEN
A Selection of *Ghazals* from his *Divan*
Translation & Introduction Paul Smith
This is the completely revised third edition of a selection of Hafiz's *ghazals*
from his Divan his masterpiece of 791 *ghazals, masnavis, rubais* and other
poems/songs. The spiritual and historical and human content is here in
understandable, beautiful poetry: the correct rhyme-structure has been

achieved, without intruding, in readable English. In the Introduction his life story is told in great detail; his spirituality is explored, the form and function of his poetry, Glossary, Selected Bibliography. 133 pages. Third Edition.

HAFIZ: THE SUN OF SHIRAZ
Essays, Talks, Projects on the Immortal Poet
Paul Smith
CONTENTS: Introduction by Richard Lee; The Life of Hafiz; Hafiz's Influence on the East & the West, The English Translations of Hafiz; Hafiz and His Translator, Sufism and God; Poetry, Life and Times of Hafiz of Shiraz; UNESCO and Hafiz; Hafiz for Our Time; Preface to Original Divan. 249 pages

~ HAFIZ: A DAYBOOK ~
Translation & Introduction by Paul Smith
Hafiz is considered by many of the world's foremost poets, mystics, artists and writers to be the greatest poet of all time. Hafiz was not only a great poet, he became a Perfect Master or enlightened being, whose wisdom and insights into the everyday and mystical path are such that it is said that one can gain spiritual advancement by reading his book. During the past six centuries he has inspired and influenced the world of literature, philosophy, mysticism and all aspects of art: poetry, painting and music in the east and the west. His life was for mankind and his work to be shared with the world. Through his example we can learn how to prepare for unprecedented change. Without doubt, he is one of the greatest human beings since time began. His *Divan* has been loved by many millions of people. To this day it is used as an oracle and spiritual guide and in this Daybook one can use his couplets on a daily basis or open them at random for inspiration and advice. 375 pages.

~˙ RUMI˙ ~ A Daybook
Translation & Introduction by Paul Smith
The great Sufi Master and poet Jalal-ud-din Rumi was born in 1207 in Balkh. Rumi's love and his great longing for the Perfect Master Shams –e Tabriz found expression in music, dance, songs and poems in his collection of poems/songs or *Divan*. This vast work included thousands of *ghazals* and other poetic forms and nearly two thousand *ruba'is* which he would compose for many years, before he became a God-realised Perfect Master himself and also afterwards. Most of the poems in this Daybook are taken from his collection of *ruba'is*, but there are also selected couplets from his

ghazals and his profound *Masnavi*. Introduction on his Life and Times, Selected Bibliography. The correct rhyme-structure has been kept in all 366 poems. Pages 383.

SUFI POETRY OF INDIA ~ A Daybook~
Translation & Introduction by Paul Smith
This is a Daybook of Sufi and Dervish Poetry of India in various poetic forms. Over 400 inspirational and spiritually helpful and beautiful poems to inspire and make your day. CONTENTS: The Poets, Sufis & Dervishes: Their Art and Use of Poetry, Glossary, The Main Forms in Persian, Punjabi, Hindi, Kashmiri, Sindhi and Urdu Sufi and Dervish Poetry of India, Selected Bibliography... THE POETS: Mu'in ud-din Chishti, Baba Farid, Amir Khusrau, Hasan Dihlavi, Lalla Ded, Kabir, Qutub Shah, Dara Shikoh, Sarmad, Sultan Bahu, Nasir Ali, Makhfi, Wali, Bedil, Bulleh Shah, Shah Latif, Ali Haider, Sauda, Dard, Nazir, Mir, Sachal Sarmast, Aatish, Zafar, Zauq, Ghalib, Dabir, Anees, Hali, Farid, Shad, Iqbal, Inayat Khan, Asghar, Jigar, Huma, Firaq, Josh. Pages 404.

~ SUFI POETRY~ A Daybook
Translation & Introduction by Paul Smith
This is a Daybook of Sufi and Dervish Poetry in the *Ruba'i* form, from the Arabic, Persian, Turkish & Urdu from Rudaki to Modern Times. 366 inspirational and spiritually helpful and beautiful poems by the greatest Sufi poets of all time including Rudaki, Mansur Hallaj, Shibli, Baba Tahir, Abu Said, Ibn Sina, Baba Kuhi, Ansari, Al-Ghazali, Hamadani, Khayyam, Sana'i, Mahsati, Khaqani, Nizami, Ruzbihan, Baghdadi, 'Attar, Auhad-ud-din Kermani, Kamal ad-din, Hamavi, Baba Afzal, Rumi, Imami, Sadi, 'Iraqi, Humam, Amir Khusrau, Simnani, Ibn Yamin, Khaju, Obeyd Zakani, Emad, Hafiz, Ruh Attar, Kadi Burhan-ud-din, Jahan Khatun, Maghribi, Nesimi, Kasim Anwar, Shah Ni'matullah, Jami, Baba Fighani, Fuzuli, Ghazali, Urfi, Qutub Shah, Haleti, Dara Shikoh, Sarmad, Sa'ib, Makhfi, Bedil, Mushtaq, Sauda, Esrar Dede, Hatif, Mir, Aatish, Zauq, Dabir, Anees, Hali, Shad, Iqbal, Khalili, Rahi, Firaq, Josh, Nurbakhsh, Paul. Sufis & Dervishes, Their Art & Use of Poetry, The Form & Function of the *Ruba'i*. Pages 390.

~ˑKABIRˑ~ A Daybook
Translation & Introduction by Paul Smith
'Here are wonderful words of wisdom (*sakhis*/poems) from one of the wisest of the wise. Here are lines of love from a Master of Divine Love, and a human being who has lived as all human beings should live, with

compassion, honesty and courage. If you want the Truth, no holds barred, it is here, but as we're told; truth is dangerous! These poems change people. You will not be the same! As Kabir says. "Wake up sleepy head!" ' From the Introduction that includes a Glossary and a Selected Bibliography. 366 wonderful short poems in this Daybook to inspire and enlighten. 382 pages.

~ABU SA'ID & SARMAD~ A Sufi Daybook
Translation & Introduction by Paul Smith
Abu Sa'id (968-1049) was a Perfect Master and a poet who lived in Nishapur and composed only *ruba'is,* over 400 of them. He was a founder of Sufi poetry and a major influence on the *ruba'i* and most poets that followed, especially Sana'i, Nizami, 'Attar, Rumi and Hafiz. Sarmad (d. 1659) was a famous and infamous Persian dervish poet of Jewish and Armenian origin. As a merchant he gathered his wares and travelled to India to sell them. In India he renounced Judaism and adopted Islam: he later renounced it in favour of Hinduism which he finally renounced for Sufism. He was known for exposing and ridiculing the major religions and hypocrisy of his day, but he also wrote beautiful mystical poetry in the form of *rubai's.* He was beheaded in 1659 by Emperor Aurangzeb for his perceived heretical poetry. This Sufi Daybook consists of 366 of their insightful, beautiful & spiritual *ruba'is,* 188 each. Introduction & Bibliography. 390 pages.

~ˈSADIˈ~ A Daybook
Translation & Introduction by Paul Smith
Sadi of Shiraz, along with Hafiz, Nizami & Rumi is considered one of the great mystical and romantic poets of Persia. His masterpieces, *The Rose Garden* and *The Bustan* (Orchard) have been a major influence in the East and West for the past 700 years. His *Divan* of *ghazals* are still much loved. His *ruba'is* have also been an influence on the poets that followed him. Here is a Daybook with a selection of 366 poems from his *ghazals, ruba'is* and *masnavis.* Introduction includes his Life and Times and Poetry. There is also a Selected Bibliography. The correct rhyme-structure has been kept as well as the beauty and meaning of these beautiful, inspirational and spiritual poems. A Daybook to remember each day. 394 pages.

NIZAMI, KHAYYAM & 'IRAQI ... A Daybook
Translation & Introduction by Paul Smith
Here is a unique Daybook of 366 poems by three of Persia's greatest mystical & philosophical poets. Nizami was a true Master Poet who is most famous for his six books in *masnavi* form: *The Treasury of the*

Mysteries, Khrosrau and Shirin, Layla and Majnun, The Seven Portraits (another Sufi classic) and his two books on Alexander. He also composed a *Divan* of approximately 20,000 couplets in *ghazals* and *ruba'is* and other forms... tragically only 200 couplets survive. His influence on 'Attar, Rumi, Sadi, Hafiz and Jami and all others that followed cannot be overestimated. Omar Khayyam was more famous in Persia as an astronomer, philosopher and mathematician... the hedonistic and occasionally Sufi philosophy in his *ruba'is* meant that his poems were never really popular in his homeland, but of course after the work of FitzGerald the west fell in love with him. He stated, "The only group which may reach God with purification of soul and renunciation of sensual preoccupations, with yearning and ecstasy, are the Sufis." 'Iraqi was the author of a *Divan* of spiritual *ghazals* and *ruba'is* and other poems and of the famous work in prose and poetry *Lama'at*, 'Divine Flashes'... a work that beautifully describes the mysteries of Divine Union that became a classic of Sufi Mysticism. The correct rhyme structure has been kept. 380 pages.

~ABU SA'ID & SARMAD~ A Sufi Daybook
Translation & Introduction by Paul Smith
Abu Sa'id (968-1049) was a Perfect Master and a poet who lived in Nishapur and composed only *ruba'is*, over 400 of them. He was a founder of Sufi poetry and a major influence on the *ruba'i* and most poets that followed, especially Sana'i, Nizami, 'Attar, Rumi and Hafiz. Sarmad (d. 1659) was a famous and infamous Persian dervish poet of Jewish and Armenian origin. As a merchant he gathered his wares and travelled to India to sell them. In India he renounced Judaism and adopted Islam: he later renounced it in favour of Hinduism which he finally renounced for Sufism. He was known for exposing and ridiculing the major religions and hypocrisy of his day, but he also wrote beautiful mystical poetry in the form of *rubai's*. He was beheaded in 1659 by Emperor Aurangzeb for his perceived heretical poetry. This Sufi Daybook consists of 366 of their insightful, beautiful & spiritual *ruba'is*, 188 each. Introduction & Bibliography. 390 pages.

ARABIC & AFGHAN SUFI POETRY ... A Daybook
Translation & Introduction by Paul Smith
Here is an enlightened Daybook of 366 inspirational poems by the greatest Arabic & Afghan Sufi poets of all time in the forms of the *ruba'i, ghazal* and others. THE POETS: ARABIC POETS: Hazrat Ali, Ali Ibn Husain, Rabi'a of Basra, Abu Nuwas, Dhu'l-Nun, Bayazid Bistami, Al Nuri, Junaid, Sumnun, Mansur al-Hallaj, Ibn 'Ata, Shibli, Ibn Sina, Al-

Ghazzali, Gilani, Abu Madyam, Suhrawadi, Ibn al-Farid, Ibn 'Arabi, Al-Busiri, Al-Shushtari, Ahmed Shawqi. AFGHAN POETS: Mirza, Khushal, Ashraf Khan, Bedil, Abdul-Kadir, Rahman Baba, Khwaja Mohammad, Hamid, Ahmad Shah, Shaida, Khalili. The correct form and meaning has been kept in all of these spiritual poems. Introduction on the Spiritual meaning of Sufi poetry and its various forms. 392 pages.

TURKISH & URDU SUFI POETS... A Daybook
Translation & Introduction by Paul Smith
Here is an enlightened Daybook of 366 inspirational poems by the greatest Turkish & Urdu Sufi poets of all time in the forms of the *ruba'i, ghazal* and others. THE POETS: Turkish... Ahmed Yesevi, Sultan Valad, Yunus Emre, Kadi Burhan-ud-din, Nesimi, Ahmedi, Suleyman Chelebi, Sheykhi, Necati, Zati, Pir Sultan, Khayali, Fuzuli, Baqi, Huda'i, Nef'i, Yahya, Haleti, Na'ili, Niyazi, Galib, Esrar Dede, Leyla Khanim, Veysel. Urdu... Qutub Shah, Wali, Sauda, Dard, Nazir, Mir, Aatish, Zafar, Zauq, Momin, Dabir, Anees, Hali, Shad, Inayat Khan, Iqbal, Asghar, Jigar. The correct form and meaning has been kept in all of these spiritual poems. Introduction on Turkish, Urdu Poetry and the Spiritual meaning of Sufi poetry. 394 pages.

SUFI & DERVISH RUBA'IYAT (9th – 14th century) ~ A Daybook~
Translation & Introduction by Paul Smith
Here is an enlightened Daybook of 366 inspirational poems in the form of the *ruba'i* by the greatest Sufi & Dervish poets and Spiritual Masters from the 9th to the 14th century. THE POETS: Rudaki, Mansur al-Hallaj, Shibli, Baba Tahir, Abu Said, Ibn Sina, Baba Kuhi, Ansari, Al-Ghazali, Hamadani, Omar Khayyam, Sana'i, Mahsati, Khaqani, Nizami, Ruzbihan, Baghdadi, 'Attar, Auhad-ud-din Kermani, Kamal ad-din, Hamavi, Baba Afzal, Rumi, Imami, Sadi, 'Iraqi, Sultan Valad, Humam, Amir Khusrau, Simnani, Ibn Yamin, Khaju, Obeyd Zakani, Emad, Hafiz. Introduction is on Sufi Poetry and on the form & function of the *ruba'i*. 394 pages.

SUFI & DERVISH RUBA'IYAT (14th – 20th century) ~ A Daybook~
Translation & Introduction by Paul Smith
Here is an enlightened Daybook of 366 inspirational poems in the form of the *ruba'i* by the greatest Sufi & Dervish poets and Spiritual Masters from the 14th to the 20th century. THE POETS: Hafiz, Ruh Attar, Kadi Burhan-ud-din, Jahan Khatun, Kamal, Maghribi, Nesimi, Kasim Anwar, Shah Ni'matullah, Jami, Baba Fighani, Fuzuli, Ghazali, Urfi, Qutub Shah,

Haleti, Dara Shikoh, Sarmad, Sa'ib, Nasir Ali, Makhfi, Bedil, Mushtaq, Sauda, Dard, Esrar Dede, Hatif, Mir, Aatish, Zauq, Dabir, Anees, Hali, Shad, Iqbal, Mehroom, Khalili, Nurbakhsh, Paul. Introduction is on Sufi Poetry and on the form & function of the *ruba'i*. 394 pages.

ABU NUWAS Selected Poems
Translation & Introduction by Paul Smith

Abu Nuwas (757-814) was the most famous and infamous poet who composed in Arabic of the Abbasid era. His style was extravagant and his compositions reflected the licentious manners of the upper classes of his day. His father was Arab and his mother was Persian. As a youth he was sold into slavery; a wealthy benefactor later set him free. By the time he reached manhood he had settled in Baghdad and was composing poetry. It was at this time, because of his long hair, he acquired the name Abu Nuwas (Father of Ringlets). Gradually he attracted the attention of Harun al-Rashid and was given quarters at court. His ability as a poet no doubt was one reason for Abu Nuwas' success with the caliph, but after a while he became known as a reprobate and participated in less reputable pastimes with the ruler. He spent time in Egypt but soon returned to Baghdad to live out his remaining years. It is said he lived the last part of his life as a Sufi and some of his poems reflect this. He is popular today, perhaps more so than he ever was, as a kind of comic anti-hero in many Muslim countries. His poems consist of *qit'as* (of which he was the first master) *ghazals* and *qasidas*. His poems could be classified into: praises (of nobles and caliphs & famous people), mockeries, jokes, complaints, love of men and women, wine, hunting, laments, asceticism. All forms are here in the true meaning & rhyme structure. Introduction on his Life, Times & Poetry and forms he composed in and an Appendix of some of the stories about him in the Arabian Nights. 154 pages.

~*NAZIR AKBARABADI* ~ Selected Poems
Translation and Introduction Paul Smith

Nazir Akbarabadi (1735-1830) is an Indian poet known as the 'Father of Nazm', who wrote mainly Urdu *ghazals* and *nazms*. It is said that Nazir's poetic treasure consisted of about 200,000 but only about 6000 couplets remain. The canvas of Nazir's *nazms* is so vast that it encompasses all aspects of human behavior and every person can find *nazms* that can suit his taste. Many of his poems are about daily life and observations of things such as training a young bear or the pleasures of the rainy season, how beauty can fade, the lives of old prostitutes, etc. His poems are loved by folk today. Many of his poems are spiritual and he is seen as a true Sufi. Bankey

Behari: 'He saw the Lord everywhere. His meditations led him to the realization of the Forms of the Lord as well as the Formless Divinity. He sings of Shri Krishna with the greatest fervour as of Hazrat Ali and the Prophet Mohammed, and turns his face if he comes across the pseudo-saints and religious preceptors who are wanting in realization and yet profess it. By far he is best in portraying the heat of his yearning for his vision.' This is the largest translation of his poetry into English, with the correct form & meaning. Introduction on his Life, Times & Poetry and on the poetic forms he used. Selected Bibliography. 191 pages.

GREAT SUFI POETS OF THE PUNJAB & SINDH: AN ANTHOLOGY
Translations, Introductions by Paul Smith
The ideal of the Punjabi & Sindhi Sufi poets was to find God in all His creation and thus attain union with Him. Thus union or annihilation in God was to be fully achieved after death, but in some cases it was gained while living. This Sufi poetry consequently is full of poems, songs, and hymns praising the Beloved, describing the pain and sorrow inflicted by separation, and ultimately the joy, peace and knowledge attained in the union. CONTENTS: Introduction: Sufis & Dervishes: Their Art and Use of Poetry... 7, Sufi Poets of the Punjab... 33, Sufi Poets of Sindh...37 THE POETS... Baba Farid... 41, Sultan Bahu... 69, Bulleh Shah... 85, Ali Haider... 113, Farid... 123, Shah Latif... 133, Sachal Sarmast... 155. The correct rhyme-structure and spiritual meaning has been kept in these beautiful, spiritual & inspiring poems. 166 pages.

~RUBA'IYAT OF IQBAL~
Translation & Introduction by Paul Smith
Muhammad Iqbal (1873-1938) was born in Sialkot, Punjab. He graduated from Government College, Lahore with a master's degree in philosophy. He taught there while he established his reputation as an Urdu poet. During this period his poetry expressed an ardent Indian nationalism, but a marked change came over his views when he was studying for his doctorate at Cambridge, visiting German universities and qualifying as a barrister. The philosophies of Nietzsche and Bergson influenced him and he became critical of Western civilization that he regarded as decadent. He turned to Islam and Sufism for inspiration and rejected nationalism as a disease of the West. These ideas found expression in his long poems written in Persian, presumably to gain his ideas an audience in the Moslem world outside India. Becoming convinced that Muslims were in danger from the Hindu majority if India should become independent, he gave his support to

Jinnah as the leader of India's Muslims. He is perhaps the last great master of the famous four-line *ruba'i* form of poetry, having composed over 550 of them in Persian & Urdu. Here is the largest collection of his *ruba'is* in English in book form, in the correct rhyme-structure and meaning. Introduction on his life, times & poetry and the form, function & history of the *ruba'i*. Bibliography. 175 pages.

~ˈIQBALˈ~ SELECTED POETRY
Translation & Introduction by Paul Smith

Muhammad Iqbal (1873-1938) was born in Sialkot, Punjab. He graduated from Government College, Lahore with a master's degree in philosophy. He taught there while he established his reputation as an Urdu poet. During this period his poetry expressed an ardent Indian nationalism, but a marked change came over his views when he was studying for his doctorate at Cambridge, visiting German universities and qualifying as a barrister. The philosophies of Nietzsche and Bergson influenced him and he became critical of Western civilization that he regarded as decadent. He turned to Islam and Sufism for inspiration and rejected nationalism as a disease of the West. These ideas found expression in his long poems written in Persian, presumably to gain his ideas an audience in the Moslem world outside India. Becoming convinced that Muslims were in danger from the Hindu majority if India should become independent, he gave his support to Jinnah as the leader of India's Muslims. In his final years he returned to Urdu as his medium with *ghazals* inspired by his on-and-off Sufism. Here is the largest collection of his poems in English in book form, in the correct rhyme-structure and meaning. Introduction on his life, times & poetry and the forms he wrote in. 183 pages.

>THE POETRY OF INDIA<
Anthology of Poets of India from 3500 B.C. to the 20th century
Translations, Introductions... Paul Smith

India has a great tradition of poetry over the past 5,500 years. From the *Ramayana* of Valmiki through to the *Bhakti* and Sufi poets and those of the recent past, its poetry is surely unique. Here for the first time is the largest anthology of all India's greatest poets, poems in the correct rhyme-structure and meaning to be studied and loved in all their beauty and spiritual significance. Here are over 100 of India's greatest poets, many of them women, including... Valmiki, Vyasa, Kalidasa, Appar, Andal, Mas'ud Sa'd, Jayadeva, Mu'in, Baba Farid, Amir Khusrau, Hasan Dihlavi, Jana Bai, Namdev, Dnyaneshwar, Lalla Ded, Vidyapati, Chandidas, Kabir, Nanak, Surdas, Babur, Mira Bai, Ghazali, Tulsidas,

Eknath, Akbar, Dadu, Rasakhan, Urfi, Naziri, Qutub Shah, Sa'ib, Kalim, Dara Shikoh, Sarmad, Tukaram, Sultan Bahu, Nasir Ali, Ramdas, Bahina Bai, Makhfi, Vemana, Wali, Bedil, Bulleh Shah, Shah Latif, Ali Haider, Sauda, Dard, Nazir, Mir, Sachal Sarmast, Aatish, Zauq, Ghalib, Dabir, Anees, Shefta, Henry Derozio, Dagh, Farid, Shad, Tagore, Iqbal, Puran Singh, Inayat Khan, Jigar, Huma. Introduction on The Main Forms in the Poetry of India. Pages… 622.

BHAKTI POETRY OF INDIA
An Anthology
Translations & Introductions Paul Smith
Bhakti is the love felt by the worshipper towards the personal God. While *bhakti* as designating a religious path is already a central concept in the *Bhagavad Gita,* it rises to importance in the medieval history of Hinduism, where the *Bhakti Movement* saw a rapid growth of *bhakti* beginning in Southern India with the Vaisnava Alvars (6th-9th century) and Saiva Nayanars (5th-10th century), who spread *bhakti* poetry and devotion throughout India by the 12th-18th century. The *Bhakti* movement reached North India in the Delhi Sultanate. After their encounter with the expanding religion of Islam and especially Sufism, *bhakti* proponents, who were traditionally called 'saints,' encouraged individuals to seek personal union with the divine. Its influence also spread to other religions. THE POETS: Appar, Andal, Jayadeva, Janabai, Namdev, Dnaneshwar, Lalla Ded, Vidyapati, Chandidas, Kabir, Nanak, Surdas, Mira Bai, Tulsidas, Eknath, Dadu, Rasakhan, Tukaram, Ramdas, Bahina Bai. Introduction on *Bhakti* & the *Bhakti* Poets of India & The Main Forms in the *Bhakti* Poetry of India. The correct rhyme-structure and meaning is here in these poems. Pages 236.

SAYINGS OF KRISHNA
A DAYBOOK
Translation & Introduction Paul Smith
These 366 wise, powerful, loving, enlightened and still totally relevant saying are from the *Bhagavad Gita,* a 700-verse Hindu scripture that is part of the ancient Sanskrit epic, the *Mahabharata,* but is frequently treated as a freestanding text, and in particular as an *Upanishad* in its own right, one of the several books that constitute general Vedic tradition. It is revealed scripture in the views of Hindus, the scripture for Hindus represents the words and message of God, the book is considered among the most important texts in the history of literature and philosophy. The teacher of the *Bhagavad Gita* is Lord Krishna, who is revered by Hindus as a

manifestation of God (Parabrahman) Himself, and is referred to as Bhagavan, the Divine One. His sayings are in answers to questions asked by Arjuna, a disciple, on the eve of a battle. "I have revealed to you the Truth, the Mystery of mysteries. Having thought it over, you are free to act as you will." Pages 376.

~CLASSIC POETRY OF AZERBAIJAN~
~An Anthology~
Translation & Introduction Paul Smith

Here is one of the few anthologies in English of the greatest poets of Azerbaijan in the classic period, from the 11th to the 17th century. All the poems translated here in the forms of the *ghazal, masnavi, ruba'i, qit'a* and *qasida* have been kept to the correct rhyme and meaning. The poets are... Qatran, Mahsati, Mujir, Khaqani, Nizami, Shabistari, Humam, Kadi Buran-ud-din, Nasim Anwar, Nesimi, Khata'i, Fuzuli and Sa'ib. There is an Introduction on Various Forms in the Classical Poetry of Azerbaijan and biographies and further reading options on all of these always engrossing and powerful, beautiful, mysterious, often romantic and spiritual and often Sufi poets. Included is the female poet Mahsati, one of the greatest poets of the east and Nizami, one of the greatest poets of all time. 231 pages.

MANSUR HALLAJ: THE TAWASIN
(Book of the Purity of the Glory of the One)
Translation & Introduction Paul Smith

The Perfect Master, poet & martyr, Husayn Mansur al-Hallaj (died 919), was born near Shiraz and was tortured and executed in Baghdad for declaring: "I am the Truth *(Anal Haq)*." Much has been written about his famous (and infamous) statement and his masterpiece *The Tawasin* in which he makes it. 'Written in rhymed Arabic prose... it sets forth a doctrine of saintship—a doctrine founded on personal experience and clothed in the form of a subtle yet passionate dialectic.' R.A. Nicholson. The Introduction here contains: The Life, Times and Works of Mansur Hallaj, The Perfect Master *(Qutub)*, 'Anal-Haq' or 'I am the Truth' of Mansur Hallaj, Four Master Poets of Baghdad who influenced Hallaj and A Selection of Poetry from the Persian, Turkish, Pushtu & Urdu Poets about or influenced by Mansur Hallaj. Appendix: The Story of Idris (Azazil) and Adam From *'The Book of Genesis'* of Shahin of Shiraz. This is a free-form poetic translation that captures the beauty, meaning, profundity of this classic of Sufism. Pages 264.

˙MOHAMMED˙
In Arabic, Sufi & Eastern Poetry
Translation & Introduction by Paul Smith
Here is a collection of poems from the time of Prophet Mohammed in the 7th century into the 20th century about him and in praise of him by some of the greatest poets writing in Arabic, Persian, Turkish and Urdu of all time, most of them Sufis. The *Koran* itself like the books of most great Spiritual Masters was in poetry as were the sayings of Jesus, Krishna, Rama, Zarathustra. There is an Introduction on Prophecy & Poetry and on the various forms of poetry used by the poets in this anthology. Included in this anthology are complete translations of the famous three *Qasidas of the Prophet's Mantle*. THE POETS (in order of appearance): Ka'b ibn Zuhair, Firdausi, Baba Kuhi, Abu Maydan, Nizami, Mu'inuddin Chishti, Ibn 'Arabi, Rumi, Al-Busiri, Sadi, Shabistari, Yunus Emre, Hafiz, Nesimi, Suleyman Chelibi, Shah Ni'matu'llah, Makhfi, Hayati, Aatish, Iqbal, Ahmed Shawqi. Pages 245.

˙˙˙GITA GOVINDA˙˙˙
The Dance of Divine Love of Radha & Krishna
>Jayadeva<
Translation by Puran Singh & Paul Smith
Jayadeva (circa 1200 AD.) was a Sanskrit poet and most known for his immortal composition, the epic poem/play *Gita Govinda* that depicts the divine love of Avatar Krishna and his consort, Radha. This poem is considered an important text in the Bhakti (Path of Love) movement of Hinduism. The work delineates the love of Krishna for Radha, the milkmaid, his faithlessness and subsequent return to her, and is taken as symbolical of the human soul's straying from its true allegiance but returning at length to the God that created it. It elaborates the eight moods of the heroine that over the years has been an inspiration for many paintings, compositions and choreographic works in Indian classical dances. It has been translated to many languages and is considered to be among the finest examples of Sanskrit poetry. Paul Smith has worked with Puran Singh's powerful & beautiful original free-form poetic version and brought it up to date. Introduction on Life & Times & Poetry of Kayadeva. Glossary. Pages 107.

ZARATHUSHTRA: SELECTED POEMS
A New Verse Translation and Introduction by Paul Smith
from the Original Translation by D.J. Irani.
Original Introduction by Rabindranath Tagore.

The Perfect Master and Prophet and one of the first poets Zarathushtra (Zoroaster) lived approx. 7000 B.C. and through his teaching of 'Good words, good thoughts, good deeds' brought in his poems that are similar in form to ruba'is a revelation and dispensation of Divinity. His teaching and poetry have influenced most religions that followed and his poems/songs were a great influence on many of the Sufi poets, including Rumi. Here are 116 of his profound, simple, inspiring poems selected from the *Gathas*. 141 pages.

THE DHAMMAPADA: The Gospel of the Buddha
Revised Version by Paul Smith
from translation from the Pali of F. Max Muller

From ancient times to now, the Dhammapada has been regarded as the most succinct expression of the Buddha's teaching and the chief spiritual testament of early Buddhism. In the countries following Buddhism, the influence of the Dhammapada is immeasurable. It is a guidebook for resolving problems of everyday life, and a primer for the instruction in the wisdom of understanding. The admiration the Dhammapada has elicited has not been confined to followers of Buddhism. Wherever it has become known, its moral earnestness, realistic understanding of human life, wisdom and stirring message of a way to freedom from suffering have won for it the devotion and veneration of those responsive to the good and the true. 247 pages

THE YOGA SUTRAS OF PATANJALI
"The Book of the Spiritual Man" An Interpretation By Charles Johnston
General Introduction by Paul Smith

The Yoga Sutras of Patanjali are 194 Indian *sutras* (aphorisms) that constitute the foundational text of Raja Yoga. Yoga is one of the six orthodox schools of Hindu philosophy. Various authorities attribute the compilation to Patanjali 2nd century BCE. In the Yoga Sutras, Patanjali prescribes adherence to eight 'limbs' or steps to quiet one's mind and liberation. The Sutras not only provide yoga with a thorough and consistent philosophical basis, they also clarify many important esoteric concepts that are common to all traditions of Indian thought, such as *karma*. Pages 173

THE MASTER, THE MUSE & THE POET
An Autobiography in Poetry by… Paul Smith

Born in Melbourne, Australia, in 1945, Paul Smith began composing poems in the ancient Persian form of the *ghazal* at the age of 6 on his way to school. Here are most of his poems composed over the past 45 years… free-form, rhyming, *ruba'is, ghazals, masnavis* etc.

Here are poems composed at home or travelling in the East and the U.S.A while giving readings of his poetry and translations. Here are poems of a personal nature, about human love & grief, about evolution and God and man and the environment and the past, present and future.

Many of the poems were composed while translating the works of Hafiz, Sadi, Nizami, Rumi, Kabir, Obeyd Zakani, Jahan Khutan and many others and while writing novels, screenplays and plays where he continued to tell the inner and outer story of his passage through this mysterious and wonderful and sometimes very painful life. 637 Pages.

PUNE: THE CITY OF GOD
(A Spiritual Guidebook to the New Bethlehem)
Poems & Photographs in Praise of Avatar Meher Baba by Paul Smith

In 1985 the author began to feel the need (usually on the site, or shortly afterwards) to put pen to paper and express in free-form, internally-rhyming poetry… a kind of descriptive inner and outer guide to each 'Baba place' in Meher Baba's birth-place of Pune, as he was experiencing it… a 'feeling' of the presence of the Master from the past that was *still available*… and, (having gone back often to many of the places and discovered this)… *the future*. He began to take photographs of the places at the same time, sometimes even in the middle of writing the poem. Interestingly, often when he read these poems to others they inspired them to visit Pune and see and experience Meher Baba's presence in these places for themselves. 159 pages.

COMPASSIONATE ROSE
Recent Ghazals for Avatar Meher Baba
by Paul Smith

While working on the *ghazals* of Hafiz and Sadi, Jahan Khatun, Nizami, Obeyd Zakani and many other Persian, Urdu, Turkish & Pushtu Poets for 40 years the author often composed *ghazals* inspired by his Spiritual Master Meher Baba. His earliest *ghazals* plus other poems inspired by him were published in the volume 'A Bird in His Hand'. The *ghazals* in this volume were composed while in India staying with Meher Baba's nephews Sohrab & Rustom Irani in Pune in 2004 and on return to Australia over the following two years under difficult health conditions. They are published here in the sequence in which they were written. 88 pages.

~THE ULTIMATE PIRATE~ (and the Shanghai of Imagination)
A FABLE
by Paul Smith

This long poem and the poems related to it were composed in 1973 while translating 'Divan of Hafiz'. The author had read Meher Baba's masterpiece 'God Speaks' that explained everything and in particular, the inner planes of consciousness... of which this is an imagined fable about such a journey. His 'Creative Imagination' at the time was so acute and deep that the journey at times seemed so real that he passed out from the bliss that he was experiencing. Since a child he had always loved pirate movies and to a certain extent in this poem he pays homage to them through the Ultimate Pirate, this time, his Spiritual Master, Meher Baba. Illustrations by Oswald Hall. 157 pages.

+THE CROSS OF GOD+
A Poem in the Masnavi Form
by Paul Smith

The masnavi is the form used in Persian, Turkish, Urdu and other poetry to write epic ballads or romances and is essentially a Persian invention. Each couplet has a different rhyme with both lines rhyming. This is to allow the poet greater freedom to go into a longer description of the subject he has chosen to present. All of the great, long, narrative poems of Persia were composed in this form that is not known in classical Arabic poetry. The most famous poems written in this form are the 'Shahnama' (Book of the Kings) of Firdausi, the 'Enclosed Garden of the Truth' of Sana'i, the 'Five Treasures' of Nizami, the 'Conference of the Birds' and 'The Book of God' and many others by 'Attar, the 'Seven Thrones' of Jami, the ten masnavis of Amir Khusraw and of course the great 'Masnavi' of Rumi. Here is a masnavi by poet and translator Paul Smith based on the following from Isaiah 53: "It is certain, the cross could not have existed without the efforts of Jesus, who is responsible for the tree, the nails & the tools that fashioned the cross; as well as the materials that fashioned the scourge, which caused His suffering." It explores with much beauty and insight the relationship between an extraordinary father and son and one's spiritual responsibility. It is a long poem for the purity inside of each of us. (7x10 inches).

CRADLE MOUNTAIN
Paul Smith... Illustrations – John Adam

In 1970 an Australian poet, Paul Smith, read in a newspaper of the death of a young fellow-poet on Cradle Mountain in Tasmania. He was deeply touched by the young man's fate and immediately began writing a poem in praise of the poet, Stephen Baxter. He contacted a friend, the artist John Adam, who read his poem and was inspired enough to illustrate it. The book was published in a limited edition to good reviews and quickly sold out. Stephen Baxter's family contacted him and told him he had truly captured the life and unfortunate death of the young poet. This newly revised edition is close to that of the original and contains all of John Adam's inspired illustrations. (7x10 inches) Second Edition.

˙˙˙RUBA'IYAT ~ of ~ PAUL SMITH˙˙˙

The *ruba'i* is an ancient form of poetry of four lines in which usually the first, second and fourth lines rhyme and sometimes with the *radif* (refrain) after the rhyme words... sometimes all four rhyme. Each *ruba'i* is a separate poem in itself. The *ruba'i* should be eloquent, spontaneous and ingenious. Every major and most minor poet of Persia and Turkey and India composed at some times in the *ruba'i* form. Paul Smith, an Australian poet, has translated all the major Sufi and other poets of this form and has composed many of his own in English over the past 45 years. Here is a large selection of his work that is at once modern and reflecting all the great Sufi *ruba'i* poets of the past. The Introduction includes chapters on his life and work, Sufism in poetry and a chapter on this popular form. Selected Bibliography. Pages 236.

FICTION

THE FIRST MYSTERY.
A Novel of the Road... by Paul Smith

THE FIRST MYSTERY is a novel that operates on a number of levels: it is a search, a tracking down of a murderer and a mystery as to who did it. It is a search through many mysterious lands, people and events. Travel Australia, Singapore, Malaysia, Thailand, Cambodia, Laos, Burma, Nepal, Tibet, Kashmir, India and San Francisco. It is a search (through dreams and visions) into the sub-conscious mind of the private detective Dave, representing the cynical westerner, who seeks but is unaware of the true nature of his journey. It is also the story of the other main characters, Johnny Wilkulda an Australian aboriginal tracker who represents the intuitive side of humankind, seeking a higher truth for himself and all others; and Robinson, the 'LSD Professor', who has taken the road of mind-expanding drugs, the 'fast road'. Meet Evie Rush, too beautiful to be a murderer? Meet Collins the murderous homicide detective; meet Arla, the beautiful jazz singer in big trouble in Bangkok; meet Margaret, haunted, looking for love in a rubber plantation in Malaysia; meet the Cambodian Prince in love with music, trying to stop war entering his country; meet Meera the Indian girl, stuck in a whorehouse in Laos and seeing visions of a new Messiah. Meet them and many other strange and fabulous, weird and wonderful characters in THE FIRST MYSTERY, a new kind of novel. 514 pages

~THE HEALER AND THE EMPEROR~
A Historical Novel Based on a True Story by Paul Smith
Monsieur Ferrier, lifelong friend of extraordinary poet, composer, linguist, author, mystic and healer... Fabre D'Olivet stands at his gravesite. Ferrier remembers Fabre's strange encounter with the unforgettable Chrisna, Le Revolution and the influence of libertines Sigault and his sister Amelie until the destinies of the future healer and emperor collide in 1800 when Napoleon seizes power and Fabre criticises him. After a bizarre assassination attempt Napoleon imprisons him. Before imprisonment Fabre has met his 'muse', the beautiful and mysterious Julie Marcel. Napoleon has married *his* muse... the older, cold-hearted and envious Josephine, 'The *only* muse in France'. After conquering most esoteric sciences and languages including the extinct ancient Hebrew, Fabre pens among many other unique works his masterpiece *The Hebraic Tongue Restored and The True Translation of Genesis*. But, to get published in 1811 he has to confront his old nemesis, Napoleon. He must prove the miraculous nature of his discovery of the essence of sound and language. He convinces a congenital deaf-mute's mother to let him try to heal him and after four days is successful! A miracle! Napoleon has him arrested after he cures another and the conflict between the healer and the emperor resumes. This time the lives and hearing of many others are at stake in this novel of an extraordinary true story! Pages 149.

>>>GOING<<<BACK...
A Novel by Paul Smith
GOING BACK is a novel inspired by a true story of love, courage and determination set in a land at peace, Australia; and a land at war... Cambodia. It is the story of people made into refugees by war: the orphans, the old, the young and those who have lost everything and the effect that

deadly landmines often have on them. It is the story of the few from America and Australia who stand up to help and love and befriend and help them. But it is mostly the amazing true story of one man who rises out of the depth of despair and through a stroke of good fortune sets off on an odyssey into a living hell and by his inventiveness and sense of humour many lives are saved and changed. Unlike other stories set in Vietnam and Cambodia that tell of war from the soldiers point of view, GOING BACK tells the tale of an ordinary man and people who act extraordinarily in the worst kinds of situations. It is a story from the recent past that could have been ripped from the headlines of today and probably tomorrow. It is an important story, a sad, funny, weird, fantastic, awful, heroic story of war and love and peace and friendship that has to be told. 164 pages.

CHILDREN'S FICTION

PAN OF THE NEVER-NEVER
by Paul Smith

Pan is awoken, after sleeping for over a 100 years, in the great wilderness of Wilson's Promontory, Australia (the real Never-Never Land) by a police helicopter searching for Brad Becker, escaped from a children's home outside Wonthaggi, operated by the abusive Mr. Harvey. Pan meets Brad who can't believe who he is but after a fast flight changes his mind. Pan needs help to dig out the lost boys old hide-out. While Brad snoozes, Pan flies over the area to check on the changes while he slept and is happy to have an encounter with the 'Pirates' motorcycle gang unloading drugs from a yacht. Pan flies Brad by night to the Children's Home to bring back Brad's friends … a new lot of 'lost boys'. But there's a snag in the guise of Sandy and Kym. Girls! The other gang members are little Danny who has discovered who Pan really is, Greg, the tractor driver; Mario, an Italian kid and Ben, an Aborigine who amazingly converses with Pan in his mother tongue. Pan flies Sandy down to check out the yacht and search for the 'Pirates' but Pan and Sandy are outsmarted and find themselves all tied up ready to become the sharks breakfast! The others break through to the "lost boys" old hide-out! They discover Pan's strange diary and flashes of his life over 2340 years open up to them as the adventure continues… but, where are Pan and Sandy? 112 pages.

~HAFIZ~
The Ugly Little Boy who became a Great Poet
by Paul Smith

HAFIZ is the true story of the ugliest boy of his age but with a remarkable memory whose father dies when he is eight and he has to live with his mother at his Uncle Sadi's house. Hafiz goes to work in a drapery shop where he becomes part of the people's overthrowing of a cruel ruler. He then becomes an apprentice baker, who delivers bread to the rich suburbs of Shiraz, Persia in 1320. One day he catches sight of Nabat, the beautiful daughter of one of the cities wealthy traders, promised to a handsome prince. Hafiz pours his love into his poems/songs dedicated to her. His words are so wondrous that the greatest minstrel of the day Hajji, takes up his instrument and serenades his loved one for him. His experiences with his Spiritual Master, Attar, and his songs and poems soon establish Hafiz as a force for truth and beauty through his beloved Shiraz, ravaged by wars and revolutions. Fame doesn't come easily as the ruthless rulers and priests conspire to silence the ever-increasing power of Hafiz's voice. Will he and Nabat and his friends like the comedian Obeyd and Hajji survive? Can words of love defeat hate's sword? Will Hafiz gain his heart's desire? 163 pages.

"To penetrate into the essence of all being and significance
and to release the fragrance of that inner attainment
for the guidance and benefit of others, by expressing
in the world of forms, truth, love, purity and beauty...
this is the only game which has any intrinsic and absolute
worth. All other, happenings, incidents and attainments can,
in themselves, have no lasting importance."
Meher Baba

Made in the
USA
Middletown, DE

77279419R00146